KEEPING

ADVENT

&

CHRISTMAS

KEEPING
ADVENT
&
CHRISTMAS

DISCOVERING *the* RHYTHMS
and RICHES
of the CHRISTIAN SEASONS

LEIGH HATTS

DARTON · LONGMAN + TODD

First published in 2017 by
Darton, Longman and Todd Ltd
1 Spencer Court
140–142 Wandsworth High Street
London SW18 4JJ

ISBN 978-0-232-53335-4

A catalogue record for this book is available from the British Library.

Designed and produced by Judy Linard

Printed and bound by in Great Britain by Bell & Bain, Glasgow

CONTENTS

INTRODUCTION

BEFORE ADVENT   9
Christ The King Sunday: Stir Up Sunday   11

ADVENT   15
Eve of Advent Sunday   17
Advent Sunday   20
St Andrew's Day   23
St Nicholas Day   27
Second Sunday of Advent   36
The Conception of the Blessed Virgin Mary: 37
    The Immaculate Conception
The Translation of the Holy House of Loreto   42
St Lucy's Day   48
Gaudete Sunday   56
O Sapienta   57
The Expectation of Mary: O Adonai   61
O Radix Jesse   63
O Clavis David   65
Fourth Sunday of Advent   66
O Oriens and Old St Thomas's Day   67
O Rex Gentium   73
O Emmanuel   74

CHRISTMAS 75

Christmas Eve 77
Christmas Day 84
Boxing Day 88
St John's Day 94
Holy Innocents 95
St Thomas of Canterbury's Day 98
The Translation of St James 106
The Holy Family Sunday 109
New Year's Eve 110
New Year's Day 113
The Most Holy Name of Jesus 115

THE EPIPHANY 117

Eve of Epiphany 119
The Epiphany 122
The Baptism of The Lord 131
Plough Monday 134

UNITY WEEK 137

Week of Prayer for Christian Unity 139
St Henry of Finland 147
St Agnes' Day 148

END OF CHRISTMAS 153

Candlemas 155
Christmas to Lent 162

APPENDICES 163

Christmas Carols 165
Bibliography 172

INTRODUCTION

Religious affairs writer Clifford Longley has observed that 'for the vast majority of those now under thirty-five, religion has no effect on their lives whatever'. In Millennium Year only eight per cent of children associated Christmas with religion and by 2004 The *Sun* declared: 'The days when Christmas had much to do with Christianity have long gone in most homes.'

'In today's consumer society,' said Pope Benedict XVI, 'this season unfortunately suffers from the contamination of commercialism that risks changing its true spirit, characterised by reflection, sobriety and a joy that does not come from outside, but from within.'

Canon Jim Rosenthal, who founded the St Nicholas Society to remind people of the origin of Father Christmas, says: 'Christian traditions, many lost over time, have such interesting elements to share and offer those wishing to mark Christmas in a spiritual and fun way.'

Dr Bill Wilson, Provost of Linlithgow in the 1970s and a life-long supporter of old local traditions, said: 'I am first and foremost a doctor of medicine and a passionate believer in preventative medicine. I observe that people are healthier, and happier - the two go together - where there is sense of community and tradition.'

Rowan Williams, soon after becoming Archbishop of Canterbury, said: 'The pressure has been to cram as much as possible into any one time, in which the divisions between work and Sabbath, labour and holiday, the seasons, even night and day, have been lined up systematically and rolled flat.' He suggests that we need to rediscover the 'rhythm of existence'.

Speaking about the Christian year he said: 'This is a path to walk year after year. You go round the story and find new things in it and in yourself. That sense of a journey through the year, through time, is to me one of the gifts of the traditional Christian year.'

The aim of this book is to show that not only does Advent come before Christmas but Christmas does not end on Boxing Day.

The liturgy in church is the apex of the church's life and anyone can participate at the parish church as much as in Jerusalem and Rome. There can also be much pleasure in rediscovering the seasonal Christian-based customs buried deep within culture and liturgy.

Leigh Hatts

BEFORE ADVENT

Christ The King Sunday: Stir-Up Sunday

Christ the King Sunday, the Sunday before Advent Sunday, is the last day of the Church year. In England it is also known as Stir-up Sunday.

Christ the King

Although this Sunday has been designated Christ the King only since 1969 it has deep biblical roots. The feast, at first observed at the end of October, was instituted in 1925 by Pope Pius XI who wished to counter the celebrations around the October anniversaries of both the Russian communists (1917) and Mussolini's march on Rome (1922) by proclaiming that there was no true king but Christ. The Pope requested that Liverpool's new Metropolitan Cathedral be dedicated to Christ the King.

It was the nature of this kingship that troubled Pilate hours before Jesus was crucified. 'My kingdom does not belong here,' Jesus told Pilate. 'You say that I am a king. I was born...to bear witness to the truth' (John 18: 37). The crown Jesus was to wear that morning was the crown of thorns. So by his sacrifice on that day, Jesus established a spiritual kingdom without boundaries. By following Christ and his teaching so room is made for his dominion.

On this day in 2002 Pope John Paul II said: 'He does not come to reign as the kings of the world do but to establish the divine power of love in the heart of the human person, of history and of the cosmos.' The Pope added that Christians should 'seek the Kingdom of God by engaging in temporal affairs and by ordering them according to the plan of God'.

The epistle reading in the Anglican Book of Common Prayer for today, the 'Sunday next before Advent', is from Jeremiah 23 and includes the words 'a King shall reign, and prosper, and shall execute judgement and justice in the earth'.

Stir-up Sunday

In that now little used Book of Common Prayer, today's collect (prayer before the readings) begins with the words 'Stir up' which gave rise to the custom of making Christmas puddings today.

> *Stir up, we beseech thee, O Lord, the wills of thy faithful people; that they, plenteously bringing forth the fruit of good works, may of thee be plenteously rewarded; through Jesus Christ our Lord. Amen.*

Stir up, or *Stiere up* as Archbishop Thomas Cranmer originally wrote in 1549, is a translation of the Sarum rite collect for the day which began 'Excita', meaning 'stir'. The prayer itself originates from the Sacramentary of St Gregory at a time when today was considered to be part of a five-week Advent. The Sarum Rite was the modified form of the Roman Mass used in the Salisbury Diocese and beyond from the 13th century to the mid-16th century.

There is no standard recipe for Christmas pudding, which has its origins in a medieval beef or mutton broth thickened with bread and enlivened by the addition of prunes (or plums) and spices. Around 1495 the meat was dropped and a stiffer mixture called Christmas pie tended to be steamed in a pudding cloth which resulted in the round pudding seen in comics and cartoons and now only sold at National Trust shops. By the mid-19th century a basin began to replace the cloth and the plum or figgy (fig) pudding, with added sugar, became Christmas pudding.

The name pudding may first have been used by Anthony Trollope in his 1858 novel *Doctor Thorne*. Bread, in the form of breadcrumbs, is still included along with the fruit in many recipes.

The Queen's Christmas pudding is made to a recipe based on one used in 1714 for George I's first Christmas in England. He was known as the Pudding King and his contained suet as well as prunes, dates and glacé cherries.

The custom of the cook inviting others to stir and make a secret wish may be an early 10th-century custom. The wooden spoon is said to represent the wood of the manger where newly born Jesus was laid. Stirring should be from east to west to signify the journey of the Magi (see page 124). Another tradition suggests that the pudding should have 13 ingredients to represent Christ and his 12 Apostles.

In Church

In the preface to the Mass, the feast proclaims 'a kingdom of justice, love and peace' which is the result of the birth, death and resurrection of Christ which has been recalled during the preceding Christian year. According to one introduction to today's Mass 'we celebrate Christ our anointed King who ... brought us out of darkness into light'. Next week, on Advent Sunday, Christians will again begin the wait in the darkness for the light of Christ.

At the climax of the Christian year the readings are a reminder that after the birth of Jesus all who follow him are part of the Body of Christ to welcome the stranger, help the poor and visit prisoners. This is Christ the servant king. The gospel reading is a passage from Good Friday when Jesus is called 'King of the Jews' or a discourse just before Holy Week on the Last Judgement.

Today is a joyful Sunday celebrating the completion of the Christian year with white vestments before beginning the cycle again with the more sombre Advent purple. Suitable hymns include *The servant king*; *Christ triumphant ever reigning*; *Crown him the Lord of Love!*; *Crown him with many crowns*; *Lord, enthroned in heavenly splendour*; *Rejoice, the Lord is King* and *Teach me, my God and King*.

Anglican Common Worship allows for a modern version of the Stir-up collect to be used as the post Communion prayer. The words *stir up*, again a translation of *excita*, will be heard again as part of the Easter Vigil collect next year.

ADVENT

Eve of Advent Sunday

Advent begins at dusk today and ends in the last hours of Christmas Eve. The earliest Advent can begin is 26 November and the latest is 3 December.

The word Advent is derived from the Latin word *Advenio* meaning 'I come'. Pope John Paul II described Advent as 'a prayerful time of waiting which prepares us for Christmas'.

The western church's four week Advent had been established by the time of Pope Gregory I in 590. But the Mozarabic rite, as found at Toledo in Spain and originally followed by Hispanic Christians under Arabic rule, still observes six Sundays whilst the Orthodox Church begins Advent on 15 November. The Diocese of Milan observes its ancient Ambrosian Rite where Advent starts on the Sunday after St Martin's Day, 11 November. Some years the Milanese can have as many as seven Sundays in Advent which is sometimes known as the Lent of St Martin.

But Advent is not the same as Lent (see page 162) although both St Egbert and St Cuthbert are known to have fasted for forty days before the Christmas celebration and the Orthodox still fast, with fish allowed only at weekends.

Advent is a time for thinking both about the birth of Christ, which will be celebrated at the climax, and the coming of Christ again. The Old Testament judgement features in the daily church readings. St Luke's Gospel quotes Isaiah's prophecy about the coming of the Messiah.

The Advent themes have traditionally been The Four Last Things: death, judgement, heaven and hell. The figures of Advent are the patriarchs, the prophets, John the Baptist who prepared the way for God to become man in Jesus and Mary who gave birth to Jesus.

Advent is a reminder that the baby in the manger did grow up and with consequences for us now. It is also the beginning of the Church year which starts quietly and reflectively although it will end triumphantly on Christ the King Sunday next year.

In Church

Evensong or vespers today is usually the first service of Advent. Tonight's vigil Mass is the First Mass of Advent celebrated in purple vestments and with the Gloria omitted.

Appropriately, an increasing number of cathedrals and other churches hold Advent carol services tonight, rather than tomorrow, with the stark Eucharist following in the daylight of Advent Sunday.

Advent Carol Service

Advent carol services increased in popularity during the second half of the 20th century. One reason is the that there was a desire to stress the Advent season and hold back the demand for Christmas carol services which now tend to be held too early in December. Many Advent carol services take the form of a candlelit Advent procession. This is a symbolic movement towards finding Christ with an emphasis of light in darkness and Christ coming soon. Through the hour-long service, the procession slowly moves down the church from west to east where Christ was born, from darkness to the brightness of sunrise.

The Light of Christ imagery of Advent and Easter Eve comes from Jesus who may have been inspired by his attendance at Hanukkah which is suggested in St John's Gospel (10.22). Some years this Jewish festival which involves the lighting of candles falls at the beginning of December.

The Procession for Advent service at King's College Cambridge was devised as early as 1934 by Eric Milner-White who recast the original Christmas Eve Nine Lessons and Carols (see page 77).

Appropriately, considering St Gregory laid down the period for Advent, plainsong (or Gregorian chant) encouraged by him is a feature of many Advent services at centres of musical excellence. Although most Advent Carol services are on Advent Eve or Advent Sunday evening there are a few held as late as the third Sunday in Advent.

Churches holding the service tonight include Christ Church Oxford, Durham, Lincoln, Salisbury, St Paul's and Winchester Cathedrals, St John's College Cambridge, Merton College Oxford and some parish churches including St Martin-in-the-Fields. Some, such as at Buckfast Abbey, begin at dusk.

St Paul's Cathedral invites its Diocese of London parishes to send representatives.

At Winchester Cathedral the service opens in near darkness with candles illuminating the choir stalls but the choristers far off singing the plainsong Advent prose.

At Salisbury tonight's Advent Procession service is repeated at the same time on Advent Sunday. At least 2,800 people attend these popular services which begin with a single Advent candle lit at the west end and culminate in 1,270 candles illuminating the cathedral. The liturgy, involving two processions moving down and around the cathedral, was developed during the 1990s by Canon Jeremy Davies and has been described by journalist Mary Ann Sieghart as 'possibly the most magical evocation of the coming of Christ in England'. Sir Robert Worcester called it 'a stunning event'.

Advent Sunday

Advent Sunday, the first full day of Advent, is the fourth Sunday before Christmas Day. Many churches have an Advent wreath, whilst homes often have an Advent calendar.

Advent Wreath

The wreath dates from 1839 when a cart wheel was hung from the ceiling of a Lutheran orphanage near Hamburg. There was a candle for each day leading to Christmas Day and by 1851 it was being decorated with greenery. Soon the idea of just five candles was adopted and by the 1920s the custom was spreading through Bavaria and Austria.

The base is a ring (representing eternity) made of evergreen (meaning beyond time). There are four purple candles (four Sundays and four corners of the earth) which are lit Sunday by Sunday until on the fourth Sunday all four candles are burning. The four can represent the patriarchs, the prophets, John the Baptist and Jesus' mother Mary. Sometimes a rose/pink candle is substituted for one of the purple ones to represent the third Sunday (see page 56). The fifth candle in the centre is white and is lit with the others on Christmas Day. The wreath is a way of looking ahead not just to Christmas but to Easter for there is sometimes a red ribbon for the blood of Christ whilst the white candle is also a reminder of the resurrection of Christ.

Most wreaths are now on a stand but York Minster has since 1994 had the largest suspended Advent wreath in Europe. The ten foot wide wreath is hoisted into position under the central tower where it remains until Epiphany (see page 117) with its candles burning all day. The wreath is lowered and raised at the beginning of the Sung Eucharist each successive Sunday of Advent for the next candle to be lit.

Advent Calendar

At home many people hang up an Advent calendar. The paper or cardboard calendar has a little door or window revealing a picture to open for each day of December until Christmas Eve.

The idea evolved in Germany from home-made count down charts with the first printed version appearing in 1903. It received a major boost on 1 December 1904 when the newspaper *Neues Tagblatt Stuttgart* gave one away with every copy. Local printers Reichhold and Lang produced its first Advent calendar in 1908 as a result of Gerhard Lang having enjoyed homemade Advent calendars as a child in the late 1880s. His first commercial calendar had little coloured pictures to be stuck on to cardboard and only later was the door feature added.

After the Second World War, which halted production and closed the firm, the custom was reintroduced in 1946 by Richard Sellmer in the living room of his house at 36 Schmellbachstreet in Stuttgart. His firm, which took the idea to America, now has a factory opposite the house producing over a hundred designs sold in several countries including the UK.

Within a few years Hamish Hamilton published the first British Advent calendars featuring a story by Dorothy L Sayers and Noah's Ark. This was soon followed in 1953 by its Enid Blyton Advent Calendar.

The present trend of having a chocolate behind each door became widespread in the early 1990s although one 1908 calendar did have sweets behind each door. A chocolate-free calendar is more in the spirit of Advent where the feast should be to come.

In Church

During Advent the priest wears purple vestments and the Gloria is omitted from the Mass. This is merely to reflect the fact that we are waiting in the dark for Christ to arrive. On Christmas Day the priest will wear white and the Gloria will be restored in celebration.

Churches now adopting the Lutheran custom of having an Advent Wreath light the first candle representing the Patriarchs Abraham, Isaac, Moses and David who looked to the eventual coming of Jesus.

Suitable hymns include *The Lord will come and not be slow*; *Lo! he comes with clouds descending,* which looks ahead to the crucifixion, *Jerusalem the Golden* and *On Jordan's bank the Baptist's cry*.

Some churches replace the appointed psalm at Mass with the Advent Prose known from its response as the *Rorate Caeli* or *Drop down dew from above, you heavens* taken from the opening words of Isaiah 45.8. The verses are derived from Isaiah 40.1; 44. 22; 65.1 and 65.10-11.

A few churches, including Durham and Salisbury Cathedrals, maintain the Sarum Rite tradition of blue vestments in Advent. Some churches veil statues of Mary holding Baby Jesus until Christmas Day. Southwark Cathedral has an empty crib during Advent.

This evening it is the custom for some cathedrals and parish churches to have an Advent carol service. (See Eve of Advent page 18.) BBC Radio 3 usually broadcasts the service from St John's College Cambridge during the afternoon.

St Andrew's Day

30 November

St Andrew's Day, which usually falls just within Advent, is significant because Andrew was Christ's disciple and associated with John the Baptist who heralded Christ.

St Andrew

Andrew was one of the Apostles. He had been a disciple of John the Baptist and was the first to be called by Jesus who saw him fishing in the Sea of Galilee. Andrew introduced his brother Simon Peter (St Peter) to Jesus and helped with the feeding of the five thousand. After Christ's ascension, Andrew is said to have preached in Greece before being martyred, allegedly upside down on an X cross, at Patras on 30 November in about the year 60. His death was ordered by the governor who was unhappy about his wife being baptised.

St Andrew is the patron of Amalfi, Barbados, Greece, Russia, Scotland, the Ecumenical Patriarchate in Istanbul and fishermen. The crest of the Barbadian coat of arms is two sugar cane stalks forming a St Andrew's cross. The world's oldest wooden building, the Saxon church at Greensted-Juxta-Ongar in Essex, is dedicated to St Andrew.

It was from a church dedicated to St Andrew and St Gregory that Augustine was sent to convert England. As a result Rochester Cathedral, founded by one of his party, was first dedicated to Andrew.

Relics

In 357 Andrew's body was moved from Patras to Constantinople where it remained until a Crusader attack in 1204. Papal Legate

Peter of Capua took care of the bones and in 1208 took most of them to today's resting place in the cathedral of his home town, Amalfi in Italy.

However, Andrew's head had always stayed in Patras. In 1462 it was given to the Pope to be with the body of his brother Peter. In 1964 Pope Paul VI returned some relics including the head to Patras where the cathedral of St Andrew now also has part of the cross on which the apostle is thought to have died. This was brought from Marseilles in 1979. In 2006 the Archbishop of Amalfi agreed to give a relic to the Church of St Barbara in Athens. An arm in St Andrew's Church at Cologne is the largest Andrew relic in northern Europe.

Some other relics, a tooth and bones including maybe three finger bones, were until 1559 at the now ruined cathedral at St Andrews in Scotland. It is claimed that the 4th-century Greek monk St Rule (or Regulus) from Patras had been told by an angel in a dream to take the relics from Patras 'to the ends of the earth' for safe keeping before the rest of the body went to Constantinople. He was allegedly shipwrecked on the Fife coast. But it is more likely that these relics came with St Augustine from Rome to England in 597 before being taken further north in 732. They may have first spent some years at Hexham Abbey which is dedicated to St Andrew. He was adopted as Scotland's patron saint in 1320 when the Pope accepted the Declaration of Arbroath asserting Scottish independence.

Now St Mary's Cathedral in Edinburgh has two relics on display in its St Andrew's Chapel. The first, believed to be a part of Andrew's shoulder, was given in 1879 by the Archbishop of Amalfi. In 1969 the second relic, a tiny piece of bone, maybe part of the skull, was handed over to Scotland's Cardinal Gordon Gray by Pope Paul VI with the words 'St Peter gives you his brother'.

In The Bible
Mark 1.16-18; John 1.40-2, 6.1-14 and 12.20-2.

In Church

A suitable hymn is *Jesus calls us! O'er the tumult* written for today by H. F. Alexander and including the words 'As of old St Andrew heard it/By the Galilean lake'.

St Andrew is not celebrated when Advent Sunday falls on 30 November except where it is the church dedication when it moves to Monday 1 December.

Today at St Andrew's Tomb

At Amalfi Cathedral, where most of Andrew's remains are buried, St Andrew's Eve vespers begins in total darkness before light from the Easter candle is passed down the church as the congregation holds candles. Incense burns in front of freestanding altar. Afterwards there is a procession to the crypt for the Miracle of the Manna. At the tomb altar, where part of St Andrew's skull is on special display, the Archbishop reaches inside to bring out a glass receptacle which is held up to show a small amount of liquid (manna) which has collected. This moment prompts a short round of applause as if to indicate relief that the miracle has again occurred.

The feast day this morning is heralded from about 3am with intermittent explosions or fireworks on the seafront. The first Mass is at 5.30am. The main Mass is at 10am attended by Scouts and town officials. As the Archbishop censes the altar he also lifts the thurible to the cross and the large silver statue of St Andrew, containing a relic, which will later be carried outside.

At about noon the statue is moved to the west door and down the 56 steps for a procession around the town's narrow streets and a visit to the beach where there is a prayer and censing. The return can be as late as 1.45pm when the statue reaches the bottom of the steps and is turned to face the crowd amid much applause. After prayers, the statue is turned back to the cathedral and carried by a crowd of young men at enormous speed in about seventeen seconds up the stairs to be received with applause, the ringing of bells and organ music.

Other Celebrations

St Andrew is patron of the Orthodox Church's Ecumenical Patriarchate in Istanbul and the Patriarch is considered to be the successor to St Andrew. The Divine Liturgy is celebrated in the Patriarchal Church of St George in Fanfar which is of special importance to the Orthodox Church since, according to tradition, the apostle was the first to preach the Christian message in and around Istanbul in the years just after Christ's crucifixion. The four-hour service is attended by a Papal delegation reciprocating the Ecumenical Patriarch's own delegation sent to Rome on 29 June for the feast of St Peter and St Paul. In 2006 Pope Benedict went to Istanbul for St Andrew's Day and in 2014 Pope Francis followed this example.

At Patras it is a public holiday and in the morning St Andrew's Cross is carried in an outdoor procession starting at the huge 1908 St Andrew's Cathedral and involving clergy and the military. The streets are decorated with banners depicting the Cross of St Andrew.

In Cologne, in the Dominican St Andrew's Church, Mass is celebrated at noon, not at the nave altar, but in the choir where the large gilded casket containing St Andrew's arm is above the altar.

At St Andrews in Scotland, where the streets are designed for medieval processions and new pilgrim routes have been devised, University students have the day off and there is often a graduation ceremony. At Edinburgh's Roman Catholic Cathedral, diocesan clergy gather for midday Mass celebrated by the Archbishop and followed by a procession to St Andrew's Shrine. An increasing number of cultural events are held to celebrate the national day which is a Bank Holiday. Appointments to the Order of the Thistle, the highest honour in Scotland and in the personal gift of the Queen, are usually announced today.

Romania recently declared today a public holiday as Andrew is an important saint for the Orthodox Church and the name day for the many called Andrei and Andrea or Andrea.

St Nicholas Day
6 December

St Nicholas died on 6 December 342 but this could be called Father Christmas's Day for he is derived from St Nicholas who was one of Europe's most popular saints and in some countries it is the figure of St Nicholas who plays the Father Christmas role.

St Nicholas
St Nicholas was born into a Christian family in 280 at Patara (now in Turkey) and became Bishop of nearby Myra, a port town known to St Luke and St Paul.

Nicholas became a monk and as an abbot performed his most famous act when giving three sisters dowries as they came of age to save them from prostitution or slavery. The tale has been rewritten to suggest that he threw bags of gold coins through a window or down a chimney. They apparently fell into stockings drying above a fireplace or shoes. This has resulted in the tradition of children hanging up stockings or putting out shoes to be filled with presents today or at Christmas.

As Bishop of Myra he was imprisoned for his faith under the Roman Emperor Diocletian but freed by his successor Constantine. In 325 Nicholas was on his way to the Council of Nicea when he supposedly performed a miracle of bringing back to life three murdered boys who had been pickled by a wicked pub landlord. This has led to the many pictures of Nicholas with babies although the story dates from a later period and the association is the result of a mistranslation.

Further reported miracles involve him appearing in a vision or dream to free three condemned men or save three storm-bound sailors. Sometimes these two stories are amalgamated.

When he died in 342 his body was probably first buried on an island off the Turkish coast. It was moved inland for safety to St Nicholas Church in Myra, now called Demre. This church, where he had served, was rebuilt in 529 but eventually an alleged threat to the body was used as an excuse in 1087 to snatch the remains from the tomb and take them by sea to Bari in Italy. This translation was arranged by Bari's Greek community who had a devotion to Nicholas. The fleet of three ships, returning from its raid on the Anatolian coast, docked in Bari on 9 May and the body was taken to St Stephen's Church where miracles were immediately recorded.

A new church where Nicholas, along with some of the sailors from the three ships, is buried was completed in 1097. The Translation of St Nicholas is celebrated in Bari with a three day festival in May. On sale is a mysterious 'fragrant myrrh', or water known as manna, which is extracted from the tomb in the crypt on the last day of the festival.

St Nicholas's life has resulted in him being the patron of bankers, single women and pawnbrokers (thanks to the three girls and the bags of gold story) children (after the pickled boys incident), sailors (following the calming of the storm) and parfumiers and apothecaries (due to the manna from the tomb). He is also patron of Russia, Lorraine, Aberdeen, Liverpool, Portsmouth, New York, merchants, scholars and parish clerks.

The earliest representation of St Nicholas is an 8th century fresco in Santa Maria Antiqua in Rome. There is a St Nicholas Chapel in Bethlehem's Church of the Nativity. Although his name was known in Saxon Britain, and Exeter Cathedral had a relic from Myra, his fame spread after the Archbishop of Canterbury St Anselm and others attended a Council called by Pope Urban II at Bari. Anselm even wrote a prayer to Nicholas. Hundreds of English churches were dedicated to him and his figure appeared in stained glass windows including one at Westminster Abbey. A late medieval window at North Moreton in Oxfordshire tells his life story.

The Saint Nicolas Cantata by Benjamin Britten and librettist Eric Crosier, first performed in 1948 and staged at this time of the year, celebrates the life of the saint who restored the pickled boys to life.

Relics

The Greek Orthodox Church of St Nicholas in Flushing, New York, was founded in 1955 and has since 1972 had some bone from the skull in Bari.

On St Nicholas day 2001, the Orthodox Bishop of Detroit received some Nicholas relics which had been in the care of the Vatican since 1453. In the same year other Nicholas relics from Rome were given to the Russian Orthodox Church in Moscow. Ded Moroz, or Grandfather Frost, a Russian Father Christmas figure appears in the New Year but is derived from the country's patron.

Even before the shrine at Bari was completed its sacristan's cousin had brought a piece of St Nicholas's finger bone to his home town of Port near Nancy in Lorraine. Now Saint-Nicolas-de-Port has the church with the tallest pillars in France and several tiny relics of the saint. After Bari this is the most important place of St Nicholas pilgrimage.

St Nicholas' Tradition

On the Eve of St Nicholas Day it is by tradition the saint who is said to visit children and leave small presents overnight in Austria, Germany, Luxembourg, Holland, Hungary, northern Italian regions, Poland and Switzerland. In some places sweets, nuts and fruit are left by 'St Nicholas' in children's shoes placed outside doors overnight on St Nicholas Eve. Around this time a figure dressed in cope and mitre as St Nicholas arrives in town centres and visits schools. In Nancy *L'Est Républicain* newspaper is full of pictures of St Nicholas visiting infant schools. At least 600 children write to St Nicholas and receive replies. Chocolate figures of St Nicholas are on sale in cake and sweet shops in early December before giving way to Christmas chocolates later in the month. The giving of presents in the name of St Nicholas began in France during the early 12th century when nuns left gifts secretly at the houses of poor people on St Nicholas Day. By the 13th century there was a tradition in Oxford of giving food to poor students on St Nicholas Day.

Father Christmas

In America a reference to the Dutch tradition by Washington Irving in his 1809 book *A History of New York* led in 1822 to Manhattan resident and divinity professor Clement Clarke Moore writing the poem *Account of a Visit from St Nicholas*, also known as *The Night Before Christmas*. This suggested that St Nicholas arrived on rooftops with reindeer and was published in the city's *Troy Sentinel* the following December. Then from 1862 the bearded figure was developed for Americans by German-born Thomas Nast's black and white drawings of Santa for *Harper's Weekly* covers and eventually he was depicted in red.

The magazine was seen in England where there was already the fictional Father Christmas featured in mumming plays and court masques. In 1616 he had appeared in Ben Jonson's *Christmas, His Masque* entertainment for James I. In 1653, having been banned by Oliver Cromwell, Father Christmas was depicted in underground literature attempting a comeback with the words 'in imitation of my great and glorious Lord and Master Jesus Christ…I come…just as my Master did not know how cruelly he would be treated'.

So Santa Claus was soon blended by the Victorians with England's Old Father Christmas to give us the present day Father Christmas wearing the red of St Nicholas.

In 1870 Macy's in New York had introduced the first in-store Santa Claus and in 1885 Father Christmas arrived at Beales department store in Bournemouth. Three years later J.R. Roberts store in East London's Stratford Broadway built a Father Christmas grotto. He did not appear at Harrods until 1908. Beales maintained the custom for over a century until 1997 with a very realistic costumed figure. From 1912 until 1965

Father Christmas had arrived at the store in a procession from Bournemouth Central Station which drew huge crowds and culminated in a balcony appearance. The occasion had all the elements of a royal or Papal visit. In the store Father Christmas was always enthroned in sight of visitors -not hidden in a grotto- and there was a post box for letters to Father Christmas which were answered.

The myth that Father Christmas lives near the North Pole, encouraged by four drawings by Nast in *Harper's* during the early 1880s, is seriously maintained. Finland has a Santapark at Rovaniemi on the Arctic Circle open all year round. In 1990 Greenland's prime minister, speaking at the Nordic Council, demanded that Finland give up its claim, adding that Father Christmas could not be Finnish if only because the language was too complicated. The Finnish reply pointed out that there were no reindeer in Greenland.

Boy Bishop

In England it is the custom in some cathedrals and churches to elect a boy bishop. This is a revival of a pre-Reformation custom when a boy was chosen to be St Nicholas, or a boy bishop, to preside over partying on Holy Innocents in the Christmas holiday week (see page 95). The election was often held just before Vespers on the Eve of St Nicholas so that during the singing of the Magnificat the bishop could leave his throne to make way for the boy bishop at the words 'He hath put down the mighty from their seats and hath exalted the humble and meek'.

This topsy-turvy tradition may be a survival of a Saturnalia custom which occurred in December involving the powerful briefly swopping places with servants. The boy bishop was provided with vestments including a cope, mitre, ring and sometimes even a chasuble although he did not of course celebrate Mass. In the early 16th century, Erasmus wrote a sermon for the St Paul's Cathedral boy bishop.

The earliest record of the boy bishop is at Rouen in the 10th century followed by Salisbury in 1222. Durham, Exeter, Lincoln and Winchester Cathedrals, Fountains and Westminster Abbeys and Beverley Minster also maintained the custom as did St Stephen's Chapel in the Palace of Westminster, Eton College and several City of London churches.

St Paul's Cathedral's 'Chyld-Bysshop', who was provided with a horse, visited Mary I at St James's Palace on both St Nicholas Day and Holy Innocents to sing with fellow choristers. The custom was banned early in her sister Elizabeth I's reign although a boy bishop preached a sermon at Chichester Cathedral as late as 1568. In France the boy bishop survived until 1721.

The restoration of the custom in the British Isles began in 1901 at St Nicholas Church in Berden, Essex. It was introduced in 1948 to St Christopher's in Bournemouth where the boy bishop made a second appearance six months later to crown the Summer Queen. Today a boy bishop is installed at St Nicholas Church at Skirbeck in Lincolnshire during an evening Eucharist whilst at Alcester in Warwickshire the boy bishop from the minster dedicated St Nicholas leads the outdoor procession during the town's annual St Nicholas Night celebration which started in 2004.

Hereford, Newcastle and Salisbury and Wymondham Abbey in Norfolk install a boy bishop during evensong on the nearest Sunday. The custom is maintained in churches dedicated to Nicholas at Bournemouth and North Walsham in Norfolk. St Nicholas's in Rossendale restored the tradition in 2007 after a twenty year break. The custom has been introduced at Claines in Worcester (1971), Mendlesham in Suffolk (1981), Fordingbridge in Hampshire (2007) and Wellingborough in Bedfordshire (2008) and Peel Cathedral (2014).

Burriana near Barcelona maintains the custom as does nearby Montserrat Abbey. At Palencia, in northern Spain, the cathedral installs a boy bishop on Holy Innocents (see page 95) and at Burgos Cathedral the boy appears on a balcony. At Legazpi, Safe, Segura, Arrasate and Zegama, in the Spanish Basque country, a boy dressed as a bishop is accompanied around the streets by young singers.

At St Mary's Church at Bucknell in Shropshire, where the boy bishop custom was observed between 1979 and 1998, there were several girl bishops. St Nicholas-at-Wade Church on the Isle of Thanet introduced the tradition in 2007 with a girl. In 2008 Rusper Primary School in Sussex elected a girl bishop with a girl chaplain followed in 2010 by St Mary's, Woodbridge. In 2014, just five years after starting the custom and weeks after General Synod opened the episcopate to women, Oldham parish church chose a girl. This is not entirely unprecedented since some convents such as Carrow Abbey in Norfolk had a girl abbess. In 2015 Salisbury Cathedral for the first time chose a member of the girls' choir calling her Chorister Bishop.

Just as some boy bishops, in St Edmundsbury and other places, once distributed special tokens which could be exchanged for sweetmeats or alms, so today's office holders often give out chocolate coins. Other modern duties can now include receiving gifts for hospital patients and presiding at a Christingle service.

A boy bishop figure was featured on one of the 1986 Christmas stamps. Some boy bishops have become priests and at least five Popes were once boy bishops.

In Church

Suitable hymns are *Good St Nicholas of Myra*; *There was a good bishop, whose story is told* and *Let us sing the song of Nicholas*, all written by James Rosenthal.

Today at St Nicholas' Tomb

In Bari, on the Italian east coast, rockets fired from the harbour pier wake the town at 4am. But many people have been up all night, sustained by polenta frittas and hot chocolate, for the first Mass at 5am in the St Nicholas basilica. The Orthodox Divine Liturgy begins at 9am at the tomb of St Nicholas in the crypt.

The main Mass is at 5.30pm when many families visit the church. At 7pm the life-size statue is carried from the sanctuary in a procession through the narrow streets of the old town, just missing washing lines, lamps and low archways. The swaying motion of those carrying the statue give it a lifelike movement suggesting that the figure is dancing to the band. It returns to the church after an hour to be greeted by applause at the west door and inside. Fireworks follow in the harbour at 8pm, sixteen hours after the first rockets were fired.

St Nicholas' Day Events

Meanwhile at St Nicholas Church in Demre, Anatolian Turkey, where Nicholas' empty tomb survives, there is in the morning an Orthodox service attended by several hundred people. The Turkish government reopened the basilica as a museum in 1981 having funded some restoration work including conservation of wall paintings and roof repairs to the partially open air building. The town square has a Santa Claus statue.

At the basilica at Saint-Nicolas-de-Port in Lorraine there is a Solemn Mass in the morning. The liturgy is adapted to include elements of an Orthodox celebration in recognition that St Nicholas is also special to the Eastern Church. The priest wears orthodox vestments, the thurible has bells attached and there is a St Nicholas icon before altar. Afterwards one can be anointed with manna from Bari. On the nearest Saturday evening there is a candlelit procession of the relics in the church which has taken place annually since 1240. During the service a 36 verse hymn is sung and there is again the imposition of manna available.

Also at the weekend, St Nicholas arrives in Nancy's Stanislas Square at the end of an evening procession of floats and appears on a balcony to a huge welcome from children and families. In Brussels, St Nicholas crosses the Grand Place on foot at the back of a procession just like a bishop except the figures ahead of him are on stilts or in a band.

At St Nicholas Greek Orthodox Church in Flushing, New York, there is Divine liturgy at 9.30am followed by a party attended by civic guests such as the Mayor of New York.

Alicante Cathedral in Spain is dedicated to St Nicholas who is the Spanish city's patron. Celebrations include a street procession with people wearing giant carnival heads and others in national costume. 'St Nicholas' rides a horse and the statue is carried at the climax. At the rear a team on a lorry give out presents. At some of the Masses preceding the feast day the imposition of the manna from Bari is available.

Significant fragments of St Nicholas' bones which did not reach Bari are beneath the high altar of St Nicholas Church on the Venice Lido where there is a special Mass.

In Amsterdam, today is often seen as the start of the Christmas shopping season. Dutch people give each other 'surprises' and hold parties and there are still some Dutch towns, such as Assan, where carols and snowy scenes in shops would be frowned upon before this date. Recently Dutch Church groups have expressed concern about the encroachment by the US-style Santa Claus.

In London the Parish Clerks Company, being the Fraternity of St Nicholas, today attends a Sung Eucharist in a City church where their banner, featuring St Nicholas looking like Father Christmas, is carried in procession. At the dinner afterwards the clerks toast each other by parish name – the clerk can represent an absorbed parish without a church of its own so the name can be a long forgotten one such as St Mary Magdalen Milk Street or St Michael-le-Quern. The Company received its charter in 1442 from Henry VI who was born on St Nicholas Day.

At about the same time in south-west London, the St Nicholas Society joins the congregation at St James's in Merton for its festival service, including special hymns and a sprinkling with Bari manna, followed by a reception.

On a Saturday before 6 December an RNLI lifeboat brings 'St Nicholas' and his helper Black Pete (usually only found in Holland) to the Harwich's Ha'Penny Pier where they are welcomed by the mayor and a band before going by carriage to St Nicholas Church for a service and distribution of sweets. The tradition started in 2005.

Second Sunday of Advent

In Church
The Advent wreath's second candle is lit to represent the Prophets Isaiah, Jeremiah, Ezekiel and Micah who foretold the coming of Christ.

The Conception of the Blessed Virgin Mary: The Immaculate Conception

8 December

This festival does not celebrate the conception of Jesus but the conception of the Virgin Mary by her mother Anne following normal sexual intercourse with husband Joachim. The announcement of the Virgin Mary being pregnant with Jesus without sexual intercourse is celebrated at the Annunciation on 25 March and also remembered in two days' time on the Translation of the Holy House (see page 42).

The conception of Mary fits in well with Advent and falls now because of Mary's birthday celebrated in nine months' time, after the normal pregnancy period, on 8 September. The confusion about the Immaculate Conception is not helped by today's Mass gospel reading being St Luke's account of Mary learning of her pregnancy from the Angel Gabriel — also read on the Annunciation. An early name for today was the 'Conception of St Anne'.

Nothing is known about Mary's parents but it is believed that their daughter's conception took place at a house in Nazareth which is now rebuilt inside Loreto's basilica where the dome frescoes include a reference to the Immaculate Conception.

Immaculate Conception

The dogma of the Immaculate Conception maintains that Mary was born free of original sin in order to preserve the purity of her future son. She was immaculate, meaning spotless and never alienated from God, because she was being prepared for her unique calling. Or as Blessed John Henry Newman said: 'She was filled with grace in order to be the Mother of God.' This reflects God's call of Jeremiah: 'Before I formed you in the womb I knew you; before you came to birth I consecrated you' (Jeremiah 1: 5 and Psalm 139). John the Baptist is said to have been born with his original sin forgiven at the moment at which he leapt in the womb of his mother as she greeted the pregnant Virgin Mary.

The idea that we are all marred by sin is an Advent theme with the coming light of Christ being both a symbol of judgement and hope. Original Sin is the bias towards sin inherited by all humans. Man is prone to evil in the constant tug of war between good and evil. There are many examples of man's inhumanity to man. So by being part of the human race we are all implicated in sin as told in the imagery of Adam and Eve. Only by following Jesus can one be redeemed and Mary was the first ahead of her son's sacrifice on the cross. It is a complex and little understood doctrine but what is celebrated today is simply the conception and holiness of Mary who, as the mother of Jesus, has such a crucial role in Christmas.

The doctrine of the Immaculate Conception was developed in Anglo-Saxon England and one of the earliest records of the Conception being celebrated is at Winchester in 1030. The Norman Archbishop of Canterbury St Anselm and the early 14th century Scottish Franciscan theologian Duns Scotus promoted the doctrine and its celebration although it was still little observed. In 1477 Pope Sixtus IV established a Mass and office to be celebrated on December 8 and this was eventually extended to the whole Western church by Pope Clement XI in 1708.

The earliest existing picture featuring the Immaculate Conception is the 1492 painting by the Venetian Carlo Crivelli now in London's National Gallery. Mary is depicted as an adult flanked by lilies for the Virgin's purity and roses for divine love. Above is God with a dove of the Holy Spirit creating the Immaculate Conception and immediately above Mary are in Latin the words: As I was conceived in the mind of God from the beginning, thus have I been made.'

After years of debate Pope Pius IX defined the dogma of the Immaculate Conception on 8 December 1854 when his Papal Bull *Ineffablis Deus* stated: '... from the first moment of her conception the Blessed Virgin Mary was, by the singular grace and privilege of Almighty God, and in view of the merits of Jesus Christ, Saviour of Mankind, kept free from all stain of original sin.'

This elevated the day, which is a holy day of obligation in some countries, whilst Austria, Italy, Portugal and Spain also keep it as a public holiday. Today is still considered to be the beginning of the Christmas shopping season in Dublin and many Italian cities including Florence, Milan, Naples and Venice. In Spain's Catalonia children know the day is special for from now they take care of a Caga Tió, a real log with a smiley face, until Christmas Day. In Panama today is Mother's Day.

In the Anglican calendar today is just known as the Conception of the Blessed Virgin Mary although some Anglican churches celebrate it as the Immaculate Conception. Pope Benedict XVI has described today as 'the entrance door to Christmas'. On this day in 1965 the Second Vatican Council concluded its three years of work.

In The Bible

Genesis 3.9-15 and 20
The passage tells the story of Adam.

In Church

Sometimes blue vestments are worn as the colour is associated with Mary. A suitable carol is *Adam lay ybounden* which emphasises original sin and mentions Our Lady.

If 8 December falls on a Sunday, then the feast is normally observed on Monday. However, some churches, especially abroad, keep it on the Sunday.

Today's Events

In Rome today is a public holiday and flowers are placed at the base of the Column of the Immaculate Conception in the Piazza di Spagna. The ancient Roman column of cipolin marble was found in 1777 in the monastery of Our Lady of the Conception in central Rome and brought to Piazza di Spagna in 1856 to celebrate the proclamation of the dogma two years earlier. The column was inaugurated by Pope Pius IX on Our Lady's Birthday 8 September the following year. Pope Pius XII sent flowers on the Solemnity of the Immaculate Conception but it was Pope John XXIII who in 1958 began the custom of the annual Papal visit.

At 7.30am today a firefighter places a wreath on the arm of the Virgin on top of the column and during the morning Conventual Franciscan Friars and Minim Friars receive and arrange flowers brought by organisations and individuals.

At 4pm the Pope arrives by car, usually passing along the Via Condotti and round the Leaking Boat Fountain at the bottom of the Spanish Steps, flanked by Babington's Tearoom and Keats House, to enter the piazza. (This can be the return route.) A huge crowd gathers early and people watch from buildings, including the Spanish Embassy to the Holy See which drapes its balconies. A litany is sung during which His Holiness presents white roses decorated with Vatican ribbon before censing the image above. The visit, which includes meeting the sick, lasts no more than thirty minutes and it is dusk as the Holy Father departs. Afterwards the friars continue to receive flowers and bouquets at the tables.

A similar tradition is maintained in Naples at 11am in the morning at a Marian column erected in 1750 outside the Gesù Nuovo, although here the firefighter on a ladder is part of the ceremony.

At Lyon in France, candles are placed in windows of houses in the old town where a procession of people carrying candles moves off from crowded St Jean Cathedral after 6pm vespers to make its way up to hill-top Notre Dame de Fourvière arriving at 7.15pm. The tradition dates from 1852 when a golden statue of the Virgin Mary was placed at the top of the little Fourvière Church bell tower which since 1883 has had the huge Basilica of

Notre-Dame added on its north side. Now the city also stages a huge three or sometimes four day Fête des Lumières featuring floodlighting and lasers.

In South America the biggest celebration is at León in Nicaragua where there is a huge novena build-up to the festival with windows decorated and flashing lights hung in the streets. Shops close at midday on the eve and at 6pm there is a procession featuring a statue of Our Lady and much lighting of fireworks by the crowd. Cheap presents, even beans and soap, are handed out by parishes and the authorities. At midnight bells ring and more fireworks are lit to herald the Immaculate Conception known as La Purísima.

Washington's Basilica of the National Shrine of the Immaculate Conception is the USA's largest Roman Catholic church and a focus today. The country was dedicated to the Blessed Virgin Mary under the title of the Immaculate Conception as early as 1792 by John Carroll, the USA's first Roman Catholic bishop, who had been secretly consecrated in Lulworth Castle's chapel in Dorset.

London's Farm Street Church in Mayfair, which opened under the title the Immaculate Conception in 1849, five years before the Pope defined the dogma, has a well-attended evening Sung Mass and party.

The Translation of The Holy House of Loreto
10 December

Today marks the arrival at Loreto in Italy of the house where Mary lived and heard from the angel that she was to give birth to the Messiah. This event is known as the Annunciation, but it is also claimed that Mary herself may also have been conceived there (see The Conception page 37).

The anniversary of the house's arrival is an opportunity to look back not just two days but almost nine months to the awesome moment known as the Annunciation. Once this was celebrated not in March but during Advent as it still is in the Ambrosian Rite where it appears on the Sunday before Christmas and in the Mozarabic Rite where the fixed date is 18 December. The Gospel reading at Mass on 20 December around this time in the rest of the western church remains the account of the Annunciation as read on 25 March.

The Annunciation
The Annunciation of the Blessed Virgin Mary, celebrated on 25 March, commemorates the day when the Angel Gabriel appeared at the home of Mary in the village of Nazareth to announce to her that she would give birth to a son called Jesus. Although still a virgin she found herself to be pregnant. The visit of the angel therefore marks the conception of Jesus whose birth is celebrated on Christmas Day nine months later, the length of a normal pregnancy.

Nazareth
The site of the Annunciation is now covered by the Church of the Annunciation built between 1955 and 1969. The remains

of Mary's house, a cave, are visible in the centre of the round basilica. The section now in Loreto was the main living area built on to the cave entrance.

Loreto

Loreto celebrates today because last night (9 December) was the anniversary of the Holy House arriving in Italy in 1294. The journey of the 23ft 6in x 12ft 10in building from Nazareth began in 1291 with a three year pause at Trsat in Croatia where there is a shrine known as the Croatian Nazareth. The sandstone and brick house without any foundations now at Loreto is encased in marble and enclosed for protection by a large church, the Santuario della Santa Casa built in 1468, just as Christ's outdoor tomb in Jerusalem is also now protected within a church.

Inside the Holy House today is the statue of Our Lady of Loreto who is reported to have appeared when the house arrived.

The house was moved by a family called Angeli which gave rise to a belief that the building was carried by angels. This has resulted not only in the charming iconography of flying and even swimming angels carrying the little house but also in Our Lady of Loreto being since 1920 the patron of pilots and air crews. Recent archaeological excavations at Loreto and Nazareth have confirmed the authenticity of the Holy House.

Pope Clement IX, inaugurating today's annual celebration in 1667, spoke of 'the Holy House of Mary, Mother of God, in which the Word was made flesh'. In the 20th century Pope John XXIII went to Loreto a week before the opening of the Second Vatican Council to pray that the Virgin would be 'the guiding star of the Council'.

John Paul II visited five times as Pope. During his 10 December 1994 visit he said that the house of Nazareth was the place where the first 'domestic church' was formed by the Holy Family. Returning to the shrine in September 1995, he said: 'We can imagine the little Jesus in his daily surroundings: while he ran and played near his home or while he slept or was sitting and eating with his parents ... (and) from Joseph and Mary he learned the most important things: humility, fidelity, prayer, work.'

At Loreto in 1939 Chiara Lubich heard the call which led her to found the ecumenical Focolare movement.

The church, containing the house where Mary spent part of her own long advent, has an Advent theme. Medallions in the nave ceiling, dating from 1492, depict the Old Testament Prophets holding scrolls of scripture foretelling the coming of Christ. The exterior of the Holy House is also decorated with figures which include the Prophets. Depicted in the dome immediately above the Holy House are both Archbishop of Canterbury St Anselm and Scottish theologian Duns Scotus (see page 38).

Buried in the basilica's Lady Chapel is poet and Loreto sub-canon Richard Crashaw who in 1648 wrote the Christmas carol *Gloomy night embraced the place*. He was in exile from Puritan England having been curate of Little St Mary's, Cambridge from 1638 to 1643.

In 2012 St Albans Cathedral signed an ecumenical link with the Basilica of the Holy House of Loreto.

Loreto Churches and Schools

Churches dedicated to Our Lady of Loreto include Our Lady of Loretto and St Michael at Musselburgh near Edinburgh where the dedication, if not the church building, dates from about 1533. A window in the sanctuary depicts the Holy House being carried by angels assisted by sea gulls. The site of the original Loretto chapel survives as a grassy mound in the grounds of Loretto School.

In England there is Our Lady of Loreto and St Winefride at Kew Gardens. Notre Dame de Lorette church in Paris, built during the 1820s and 1830s, is well-known for the Lorette metro station alongside. The USA has a large number.

The Loreto Sisters, who run schools in several countries, were formed by Frances Ball, a member of the Institute of the Blessed Virgin Mary, who in 1822 returned home to Ireland to establish a convent in a Dublin house she named Loretto House because IBVM founder Mary Ward (1585-1645) had a great devotion having visited the Holy House in 1621.

Holy House Replicas

There are replicas of Mary's house, based on Loreto, in six churches in Italy: Aversa, Parma, Catania, San Clemente Venice, San Pantalon Venice and Vescovana. There are also several in the Czech Republic, including an impressive outdoor copy in Prague. Poland has a Shrine of the Holy House at the Franciscan Church in Głogówek and a freestanding one in Golab.

Glastonbury Abbey in Somerset had one built about 1520 by Abbot Richard Beere who had been to Loreto but just over a decade later it was destroyed. However, the first Holy House at Walsingham in Norfolk was built before the original's translation from the Holy Land.

Walsingham

In 1061 Walsingham's lady of the manor Richeldis had a vision of Our Lady directing the building of a copy of the house where she had heard that she was to be the Mother of God. The small Holy House was built in Saxon style (wood, wattle and daub) to the dimensions given. Excavation has found a building of the same width as Loreto's but eight foot shorter. As it became a place of pilgrimage so it was protected with stone. This Holy House was destroyed in 1538 but today there is another, built only in 1931, at the instigation of the Vicar of Walsingham Alfred Hope Patten. He had been curate at St Mary's, Buxted in Sussex where the church, opened in 1887, has a Lady Chapel built to the dimensions of Walsingham's Holy House. Nazareth's Church of the Annunciation has a large mosaic of Walsingham.

In The Bible

Matthew 1.18-23 and Luke 1.26-58

Mary was in her house at the then southern end of Nazareth when the angel Gabriel appeared and told her that she would give birth to a baby to be called Jesus. Mary, a virgin frightened by the angel and the message, heard that her son she was already carrying would have 'the throne of his ancestor David' (a reference to Mary's husband Joseph who was a descendant) and that 'his reign will have no end'. The angel added that her cousin Elizabeth was already six months pregnant. Mary replied: 'I am the handmaid of the Lord. Let what you have said be done to me.'

Meanwhile Mary's pregnancy came as a shock to Joseph who initially decided to quietly seek a divorce. (Girls were sometimes betrothed as young as 12 in advance of living with the husband.) However his mind changed when an angel appeared to him in a dream to confirm the unprecedented virgin birth situation and foretell that Jesus will 'save his people from his sins'.

During her pregnancy, Mary went to stay with Elizabeth who was about to give birth to John the Baptist, Jesus' forerunner (see Baptism of The Lord page 136).

In Church
Today is celebrated as the Translation of the Holy House or Our Lady of Loreto in many churches including those in Italy, where today is known as Madonna di Loreto.

Collect

O God, who through the Mystery of the Word made flesh, didst in Thy mercy sanctify the House of Blessed Mary the Virgin, and by wondrous means didst place it in the care of Thy Church, grant that we may keep aloof from the tabernacles of sinners, and become worthy habitants of Thy holy house. Through the same Christ our Lord, Amen

Readings

Is 7.10-14; Revelation 21. 1-5; Luke 1.21-38.

Post-communion Prayer

Lord God, in this commemoration of Our Lady of Loreto, you have given us a share in your redemption. Grant that we may enjoy your fullest blessings and experience ever more fully the mystery of our salvation.

Today at Loreto

Crowds build in the afternoon of the eve on 9 December when, outside one side of the walled hilltop town, a market sells mainly food. By tradition the evening sees bonfires lit in the surrounding countryside supposedly to guide the angels with the holy house. The occasion is known as festa della venuta meaning feast of the arrival. At 9pm there is a Solemn Mass and outdoor procession with a statue of Our Lady of Loreto. People arrive for this, the festival's main event, from 6pm when the church doors open for vespers. Before 8pm every seat, step and corner is taken and the last hour of waiting is spent in rehearsing the much loved music in which the congregation fully participates. The Mass is broadcast on television and so screens in church and outside enable everyone to see the sanctuary.

Some seats are reserved for the Air Force who carry the statue in procession during the singing of the Loreto Litany, approved by Pope Sixtus V in 1587, which can feature forty-eight titles for Mary.

The appearance of the statue is by tradition met with the waving of white handkerchiefs inside and outside the church. The celebration ends by midnight.

This morning the main event is a sung Mass at 11am when the Air Force members in uniform provide the crucifer, acolytes and thurifer for the serving team as well as readers. On both days there are long queues outside the Holy House.

Other Celebrations

At Church of Our Lady of Loretto and St Michael, in Musselburgh, there is a morning Mass. On the second or third Sunday of Advent the main Mass includes a hymn to Our Lady of Loretto, *Wond'rous the throne from which Gabriel came*, written and composed by Roy and Catrina McGillivray.

St Lucy's Day

13 December

St Lucy suffered martyrdom on this day in 304 during the rule of the Roman Emperor Diocletian under whose laws St Nicholas (see page 27) was later imprisoned. In the calendar Lucy has become a female companion to Nicholas although St Lucy's Day is mainly celebrated in Sicily and Sweden. In Sweden she is a symbol of the light of Christ celebrated at Christmas.

St Lucy

Lucy lived in Siracusa, a port in Sicily where St Paul had spent three days on his way from Malta to Rome (Acts 28.12). Her wealthy father died when she was five. As a young woman in 301 she took her sick widowed mother to nearby Catania to pray for a cure at St Agatha's tomb. There they fell asleep and in a dream the saint told Lucy that she and her mother should sell their goods and give the proceeds to the poor. This they eventually did but their action aroused the fury of Lucy's suitor who gave evidence against her during a persecution of Christians ordered by the Emperor.

Lucy refused to renounce her faith, became immovable when ordered to a brothel and was killed with a sword in the neck.

The oldest picture of Lucy is a 6th-century mosaic in Ravenna's Basilica of Sant' Apollinare Nuovo. Due to a tradition that her eyes were torn out she is often depicted with her two eyes on a dish.

The modern depiction of her wearing a crown of lighted candles is derived from the claim that she led persecuted Christians to safety through catacombs by lighting the way with candles on her head whilst her hands were full of food for the fugitives.

It was only a short time before Lucy had an honoured place among the saints, a church dedicated to her in Rome and by 604 her name was included in the canon of the Mass. Her fame was spread in the very early 8th century by St Aldhelm, Bishop of Sherborne, who wrote about her good deeds and martyrdom.

The site of her death in Sicily is now covered by St Lucy's Church where Caravaggio's painting *The Burial of Saint Lucy* hangs behind the altar. He painted it whilst in Siracusa during November 1608 to be ready for her feast day the following month. He intended that the light from the west end rose window would draw attention to Lucy's face making her the focus of the scene and a representation of light shining through darkness.

A tunnel leads from the church to a nearby round chapel sunk into ground to embrace the catacomb where she was buried. It was from this tomb that the body was taken to Constantinople in 1039. The body arrived in Venice in 1204 and from 1313 was at a Santa Lucia church fronting the Grand Canal in the Cannaregio district. When this church was demolished in 1864, to make way for the Venezia Santa Lucia railway station piazza, the remains were moved to nearby San Geremia where her clothed body now lies in a glass sarcophagus behind the altar. Her hands and feet are exposed but since 1955 her face has been hidden by a silver mask at the request of the future Pope John XXIII who was then Patriarch of Venice.

In 1981 her body was stolen in an armed raid during which the skull fell on the floor to be left behind by the robbers who later demanded a £100,000 ransom. The body was found on St Lucy's Day in a nylon bag and she was restored to her shrine wearing a new dress.

In 2004, the 1700th anniversary of her death, the body was taken by air and sea to visit Siracusa on her feast day.

Lucy is the patron of opticians, blind people, photographers and Sweden. England has ancient church dedications to her at Dembleby in Lincolnshire and Upton Magna near Shrewsbury. In 1976 a church dedicated to St Lucy opened in Scotland's Cumbernauld to serve the new Abronhill housing estate. The cathedral at Kotahena in Sri Lanka is also dedicated to her.

Swedish Sankta Lucia Ceremonies

The name Lucy is derived from the Latin word *lumen* meaning 'light'. In Sweden the use of candles, on one of the shortest days in the year, is taken as a symbolic glimpse of the greater light to come at Christmas. Until the change of calendar, today was the shortest day of the year as recorded by Dean of St Paul's John Donne (1572-1631) in his poem *A Nocturnal Upon St Lucy's Day* which begins "Tis the year's midnight…'.

The Sankta Lucia tradition in Sweden can be traced back to 1764 although some parts of Sweden had long kept the eve of the 13 December with a meal called *att lussa* served by candlelight during the long cold night.

In many Swedish family homes, the youngest daughter will get up just before first light and put on the traditional white dress with a red or blue sash. She places on her head a crown of lingonberry twigs with nine lighted candles —which now tend to be battery operated for safety— and carries a tray of coffee and saffron bread called Lussikatter (Lucy cats) since the golden rolls with a raisin for an eye represent evil cats supposedly subdued by Lucy. Outside her parents' bedroom door she begins in Swedish the Sankta Lucia (pronounced loo-seer) song:

> *Darkness is all around*
> *Deep shadows linger.*
> *But when you hear the sound*
> *of a white clad singer,*
> *Out of the frosty night*
> *steps our maid of light:*
> *Santa Lucia! Santa Lucia!*

The Lucia song was brought from Naples to Sweden in the mid-19th century by composer and poet Gunnar Wennerberg. The original text, first published in 1848, is about a little fishing port Santa Lucia which is now part of Naples. The small St Lucy church, now a landlocked basilica but still known as the Basilica di Santa Lucia a Mare (by the Sea), stood on the seaward edge of the quay with the sea lapping its 'east' end. The song was a fisherman's invitation to board his boat and enjoy the view of the city as the sun sets. Caruso, Pavarotti, Perry Como and Elvis Presley all recorded the song.

The tradition of Swedish towns, schools and churches electing their own young girl to be Lucia began in 1927 when a Swedish newspaper *Stockholmstidningen* organised a contest and crowning.

The Lucia Celebrations in church take the form of a series of folk songs and maybe carols with a reading. Lucia enters and departs to the Lucia song. Sometimes she is accompanied not only by female attendants in white but also by star boys, carrying a large star on a pole. This is really the transfer of an old Epiphany tradition (see page 128) known in Germany and the east to give young males a role.

The only relic of St Lucy in Sweden is a sliver of bone given to the ancient church on Frösön Island in Lake Storsjön.

In The Bible
St John 1.5 and 8.12
According to the prologue to St John's Gospel Jesus is 'a light that shines in the dark'. When teaching Jesus said: 'I am the light of the world: anyone who follows me shall not be walking in the dark; but will have the light of life.'

In Church on St Lucy's Day
The vestments are red. A suitable prayer is the one composed in 1957 by Pope John XXIII:

> *O glorious Saint Lucy, who in the time of trial, professed*
> *your faith and accepted martyrdom. Obtain for us the grace*
> *to profess the truths of the Gospel and to continue in faith*
> *according to the teachings of Our Saviour.*
> *O Virgin of Syracuse,*
> *be the light in our lives and model in every action,*

so that, after having imitated you in this world we may,
with you, rejoice in the vision of God.
Amen.

Today prayers are said for blind people and those who help the blind; opticians and also photographers, especially those in the press who have the responsibility of bringing pictures to others.

The RC Eucharistic Prayer 1, the prayer of consecration in the Mass written by St Gregory and based on an earlier version, mentions St Lucy.

Today at St Lucy's Tomb

In Venice the church of San Geremia e Lucia, where the body of St Lucy rests, is open from 7am to 8.30pm with bell ringing marking the opening and closing. The presence of candle sellers outside reminds passing commuters from the station that it is 'Santa Lucia' Day. There are Masses on the hour from 8am to 7pm with two in the afternoon attended by optometrists and opticians and blind people. The main celebration is at 5pm when the Patriarch arrives by barge to preside and blind people read and lead the prayers. At the end the clergy carry small candle lights to the shrine where the body is censed and the blessing given. Visitors call in all day to light candles with the first arrivals being the night before at the 6pm vigil Mass. Floral decorations at the shrine include a huge bouquet from the Venetian opticians. A candle is sent from Lucy's home city of Siracusa.

Today at St Lucy's home and martyrdom

In Siracusa preparations begin on 30 November when the doors in the cathedral's St Lucy Chapel, normally partly covered by a painting of Lucy, are opened to reveal the almost life-size 16th-century silver statue of the saint. At 11.30am on St Lucy's eve the statue is slowly and with difficulty moved to above the High Altar. At 7pm there is vespers and Mass. Afterwards Cuccia, a sweet mixture of cheese, chocolate, fruit and wheat in foil cups, as well as St Lucy bread rolls, are distributed to the huge congregation leaving the cathedral.

Cuccia, pronounced *koo-chi-ya*, is a creamy pudding sold at this time in bakers' shops. It has various recipes which sometimes include crystalized fruit, ricotta cheese and even salt. But the base is always wheat to recall the ship which arrived with welcome wheat in 1646 after Siracusans had asked Lucy to intercede for them at a time of famine.

Also eaten throughout Sicily today is Arancini, meat in rice balls coloured with saffron.

Today at 10.30am there is a solemn Mass in the cathedral attended by dignitaries. At 3.30pm the statue, which contains three of Lucy's ribs, is carried by 60 bearers from the cathedral through cleaned streets and past decorated balconies to the Santa Lucia basilica outside the old town. In front are women carrying some of her relics returned to Siracusa. Fireworks used to be let off as the statue left the cathedral in daylight and again in darkness as it left the Ortygia, the old island city, at the bridge but since 2012 churches tend to ring bells instead. The procession is preceded by hundreds of women, some barefoot, carrying long candles and often accompanied by family and friends. In 2013 the number of people accompanying the statue was 35,000, the highest figure since 1988 when the Patriarch of Venice brought a relic as a gift. After about five hours, the bell rings out at St Lucy's as the statue approaches carried by the exhausted bearers who have had many pauses.

At the basilica, on the martyrdom site, the statue is lifted above the altar where a canopy has been erected masking the Caravaggio painting. The church is always packed whilst outside a huge crowd watches the arrival and enjoys the fair in the piazza. Many take the opportunity to visit the nearby Sepolcro, Tomb Church, on her anniversary.

The statue remains for eight days, the octave, before starting its return at 4pm on 20 December and, having paused just below the hospital's department of ophthalmology, arriving back about 9.30pm on the eve of the shortest day.

In 2014 St Lucy's body, which had been flown from Venice just after her feast day for a second time after a decade, was carried for the first time in the return procession which is always joined by Sweden's National Lucia.

Other celebrations

In Stockholm, the National Lucia, the winner of a contest organised by a magazine, this evening takes part in a carriage procession from Nordiska Kompaniet department store to Skansen for an outdoor Lucia celebration. Celebrations are held in the cathedral and city centre churches such as St Jacob's in the early evening. Choirs are often provided by students from the famous Adolf Fredrik Choir School.

The custom was adopted by Denmark in 1944 following the Second World War and came to Finland in 1950 when it was introduced by Finland's principal Swedish-language newspaper and the health organisation Folkhälsan. The custom has now spread to the families of the Finnish-speaking majority. Finland's National Lucia is chosen from teenage girls by public vote which is combined with fund raising for the Folkhälsan health care programme. This evening there is the Santa Lucia coronation in Helsinki Cathedral broadcast on a giant screen outside. The young woman, wearing a crown of lighted candles and carrying a wheatsheaf, appears on the cathedral steps and then rides in a horse-drawn carriage procession to the Market Square. During the rest of December she pays visits to hospitals and schools.

In Naples' Lucia church the day starts at 5.45am with fireworks in the street before the first of eight morning Masses. So crowded is the building that there is a one-way route round the church all day. After a Solemn Mass in the evening there are more fireworks outside the main entrance.

On the island of Gran Canaria's Santa Lucia de Tirajana village, a fiesta has since 1967 featured both a Swedish girl with a candle crown and a Canarian girl in a tiara representing St Lucy. After Mass in church they both walk behind the statue in an outdoor procession.

There are many St Lucy fairs across Europe. At Lecce in Puglia, Italy, a St Lucy Fair, which runs until Christmas Eve and until recently started today, sells crib figures made of clay and papier mache crib scenes.

At Barcelona in Spain there is a constant stream of people visiting the St Lucy Chapel in the cathedral to have their eyes blessed and venerate a Lucia relic. The little 13th-century chapel, entered from the street, is cleared of pews for the occasion. Flowers pile up on the altar. Pilgrims exit into the cloister where lighted candles multiply on stands and steps. The chapel is open on the previous evening and all day from 7am to 8pm although the doors may close a little later. The numbers are so great that barriers are set up outside to contain a queue. Meanwhile the Fira de Santa Llúcia (or St Lucy Market) takes place outside, as it has since 1786, selling crib items. Here Lucy is the patron of both blind people and fashion designers. In Catalonia it was the custom for student seamstresses to go round the streets singing and collecting money. Sometimes one was dressed as St Lucy by wearing a crown of flowers.

Lucy is patron of ONCE, Spain's national organisation for blind people known for its weekly lottery, which was founded on 13 December 1938.

In London there is a Lucia celebration in either St Paul's Cathedral or Westminster Cathedral in a tradition begun in 1990 by London's Swedish congregations. More recently it has become an annual occasion at Southwark Cathedral. Since 2013 there has been one at York Minster. Other major UK cities also have celebrations around this date.

The Caribbean island of St Lucia, a member of the Commonwealth with the Queen as head of state, is named after St Lucy and today celebrates its national day with a festival of lights. French sailors shipwrecked on the island on 13 December 1502 are believed to have named the island St Lucia.

In Croatia today wheat seeds are planted in a dish of soil indoors and watered daily until Christmas Day when Lucy Wheat shoots are placed next to the manger or used a table decoration.

Gaudete Sunday
Third Sunday of Advent

The third Sunday in Advent is widely known as Gaudete Sunday which means Rejoice Sunday. It takes its name from the words of the entrance antiphon, or introit, at the beginning of Mass, 'Rejoice in the Lord always; again I say, rejoice! Indeed, the Lord is near' (Philippians 4: 4-6). There is a sense of rejoicing because we are halfway through Advent and Christmas is nearer.

In Church

The vestments are pink. In the past they would have been more pink-purple rather than pink-red. Bright pink only dates from the invention of synthetic dyes. This custom imitates Lent when in the middle, Mothering Sunday, there is some rejoicing and the vestments change just for one day from purple to rose.

The Advent wreath's third candle, which may be pink like the vestments, is lit to represent John the Baptist, who was the forerunner of Christ and baptised Christ.

The readings and psalms appointed for today have the theme of joy and rejoicing.

Other Events

In Rome there is always a larger than usual crowd in St Peter's Square at noon for the blessing of the 'Bambinelli'. After the Pope has led the Angelus from his window he gives a blessing of Baby Jesus figures held up by children and destined to be placed in home, school or parish nativity scenes.

O Sapienta

17 December

Today the Advent mood changes as, whilst still looking to Christ's promised second coming, the focus turns towards the celebration of Christ's first coming in the stable at Bethlehem.

The name for today, O Sapientia, is found in some calendars but rarely is there an explanation. 'Oh Sapienta', meaning 'O Wisdom', is the opening of the ancient antiphon used at services today.

O Antiphons

This is the first of the seven O Antiphon days when the Messiah is called by an ancient title. Mary and Joseph are said to have set out today from Nazareth on their 90 mile journey to Bethlehem which they reach on 24 December. It was once the custom in monasteries to toll the loudest bell as each antiphon was sung over the coming days to remind people that Mary and Joseph were on their way.

'What was born in Bethlehem was the Wisdom of God,' said Pope Benedict XVI when presiding at tonight's Vespers in 2009. 'In the fullness of time this Wisdom assumed a human face, the face of Jesus.' The antiphons begin to explain who the Messiah is.

Before Advent existed, today was the start of preparation for Christmas and Epiphany. The Synod of Zaragossa in 380 had obliged the faithful to fast and be in church daily from the 17 December to 6 January which coincided with the pagan Saturnalia.

The O Antiphons, or seven Great Advent Antiphons, date from the 8th century with the earliest reference being found in Anglo-Saxon England. They are mainly a compilation of sometimes recurring titles for Christ from the prophecy of Isaiah in the Old

Testament expressing both the hope for the birth of the Messiah and today's longing of Christians to celebrate Christ's birthday. Each one starts with an acclamation of a title for the coming Messiah and ends with a request to God. The antiphon frames the Magnificat at evensong and is now also heard at Mass.

The Mozarabic Rite maintained in Toledo has just a long O after the Magnificat to express the intense longing for the coming of Christ.

The Antiphons were first translated from Latin into English by Blessed John Henry Newman. The various and often beautiful translations used today can be found in Common Worship, New English Hymnal, the Missal and the Breviary.

O Sapienta

O Wisdom, you came forth from the mouth of the Most
  High,
reaching from end to end to the other mightily,
and sweetly ordering all things:
Come and teach us the way of prudence.

(Common Worship)

'Wisdom I loved and searched for from my youth'

(Wisdom 8.1)

'I came forth from the mouth of the Most High,
and I covered the earth like mist'

(Ecclesiasticus 24.3)

'On him will rest the spirit of Yahweh,
the spirit of wisdom and insight ...'

(Isaiah 11.2)

'All this is a gift from Yahweh Sabaoth,
marvellous advice (or wisdom) leading to great achievements.'

(Isaiah 28.29)

16 or 17 December

The 16 December, as indicated in the Book of Common Prayer, was once the first day of the O Antiphons because for a time there was an eighth antiphon – O Virgin of Virgins – sung on 23 December. This extra one was officially dispensed with in 1568 although its usage lingered on in England and in Spanish speaking countries. Today Salisbury Cathedral retains the eight antiphons and so begins on 16 December.

A window, by Paul Franz Bonnekamp, installed in 1960 at St Foillan Church in Aachen features the seven O Antiphons.

In Church

In order to be heard by a wider number of Christians, the O Antiphons now also appear in modified form in the Mass as the Acclamation before the gospel reading.

Today the preface at Mass (immediately before the Sanctus or Holy, Holy, Holy…) changes to include references to the Virgin Mary and John the Baptist. This is repeated daily until Christmas.

The Gospel passage at today's Mass is a rare reading the genealogy of Jesus (at the beginning of St Matthew's Gospel) which makes a link from the Old to New Testament and involves a collection of good and bad people through whom God worked to bring us Jesus. It seeks to confirm that through Jewish law Jesus is connected to the royal line of David and great leaders and will himself call and work through a diverse number of people. This reading, heard also on Our Lady's Birthday on 8 September, is repeated at the vigil Mass on Christmas Eve. After today the daily Gospel readings are the infancy narratives.

The antiphon is sung at evensong and vespers before and after the Magnificat, Mary's revolutionary song. Composer Bob Chilcott has produced a new setting for the antiphons.

The Advent hymn *O come, O come, Emmanuel* is a translation by J.M. Neale of a hymn *Veni, veni Emmanuel* sung in Cologne with verses based on five of the Advent Antiphons. It first appears in a 1710 prayer book but the tune is a 15th-century funeral litany from a Franciscan convent in Lisbon.

Today's Events

Las Posadas

Las Posadas – meaning lodgings or the inns – begins in Mexico on the old date of 16 December. Every evening for nine days, processions re-enact Mary and Joseph's search for a bed. Each night a different home hosts a party with a family playing the part of the inn keeper and the guests, including children carrying small statues of Mary and Joseph, singing a song requesting lodging. Guests go in a candlelit procession first to two houses where they are by arrangement refused hospitality before arriving at the house designated as that night's inn and the party venue.

St Mary Magdalene's in Millfield, Sunderland, was one of the first British churches to have a posada with the church's Mary and Joseph crib figures staying at a different house in the parish every night between Advent Sunday and the Fourth Sunday of Advent. Edinburgh's Episcopal Cathedral adopted the custom in 2010 with two specially carved stone figures of Mary and Joseph which move from family to family to arrive back in the Cathedral for Christmas Eve's Crib Service.

Rooster's Mass

Misa de Gallo meaning 'Rooster's Mass', nine days of pre-dawn celebrations, begins in the Philippines on 16 December and continues until Christmas Eve. The alternative Filipino name is *Simbang Gabi* or 'Night Mass'.

The Expectation of Mary: O Adonai

18 December

The Expectation of Mary

In Spain and some other countries, today is known as the Expectation of Mary. Its origin lies in a decision taken in Toledo in 656 to observe the Annunciation today rather than on 25 March because it fell in Lent. This remains the situation for the Mozarabic Rite followed in Toledo although of course the rest of the Spanish Church keeps the Annunciation in March. The Annunciation can now be handily recalled on 10 December (see page 42).

But today, also called Our Lady of the O (Nuestra Señora de la O) because of the O Antiphons, remains an occasion to highlight Mary's pregnancy. In the cloister of Madrid's Real Monasterio de la Encarnación (the convent dedicated to the Incarnation of Christ) there is a painting depicting Mary, with the Christ Child in her womb, surrounded by the words of the O Antiphons which climax with a supplication to the Child.

O Antiphon

Today's antiphon is O Adonai.

> *O Adonai, and Leader of the house of Israel,*
> *you appeared to Moses in the flame of the burning bush*
> *and gave him the law on Sinai:*
> *Come and redeem us with an outstretched arm.*
>
> (Common Worship)

'The angel of Yahweh appeared to him in a flame blazing from the middle of a bush.'

(Exodus 3.2)

'Yahweh said to Moses, "Come up to me on the mountain. Stay there, and I will give you the stone tablets -the law and the commandment- which I have written for their instruction".'

(Exodus 24.12)

Adonai is Hebrew meaning 'Lord' or 'Ruler' and, because of its sacred character, is replaced in public readings by Yahweh, another Hebrew word for God.

In Church

The O Adonai antiphon precedes the Gospel at Mass and bookends the Magnificat at evening prayer.

O Radix Jesse

19 December

Today's antiphon is O Radix Jesse.

O Root of Jesse, standing as a sign among the peoples;
before you kings will shut their mouths,
to you the nations will make their prayer:
Come and deliver us, and delay no longer.

(Common Worship)

'A shoot springs from the stock of Jesse.'

(Isaiah 11.1)

'That day, the root of Jesse, standing as a signal for the
peoples,
will be sort out by the nations ...'

(Isaiah 11.10)

'... kings will stay tight-lipped before him.'

(Isaiah 52.15)

Jesse was the father of King David and from his line it is suggested that Jesus will come. This is referred to by St Paul (Romans 15.12). St Matthew starts his Gospel (read two days ago on the first day of the Advent Antiphons) with an extraordinary attempt at a family tree containing many diverse people including Jesse and ending with Jesus' stepfather Joseph.

In Church

The O Radix Jesse antiphon precedes the Gospel at Mass and bookends the Magnificat at evening prayer.

O Clavis David

20 December

Today's O Antiphon is O Clavis David:

O Key of David, and sceptre of the house of Israel;
you open and no one can shut;
you shut and no one can open:
Come and lead the prisoners from the prison house,
those who dwell in darkness and the shadow of death.

(Common Worship)

'I shall place the key of David's palace on his shoulder;
when he opens, no one will close,
when he closes, no one will open.'

(Isaiah 22.22)

'…to free captives from prison,
and those who live in darkness from the dungeon.'

(Isaiah 42.7)

In Church

The O Clavis David antiphon precedes the Gospel at Mass and bookends the Magnificat at evening prayer.

Fourth Sunday of Advent

In Church

This Sunday is a preparation for Christmas. The Advent wreath's fourth candle is lit to represent Mary. This custom maintains an old tradition of Mary being remembered around this time of the Feast of the Expectation of Mary.

A suitable hymn is *O come, O come, Emmanuel* (see page 59).

O Oriens
Old St Thomas's Day
21 December

Today's O Antiphon is O Oriens:

O Morning Star;
splendour of light eternal and sun of righteousness:
Come and enlighten those who dwell in darkness
and the shadow of death.

(Common Worship)

'The people that walked in darkness has seen a great light;
on inhabitants of a country in shadow dark as death
light has been shined.'

(Isaiah 9.1)

'... a star is emerging Jacob ...'

(Numbers 24.17)

The star imagery is suitable for today which is now, following the change in calendar, the shortest and so darkest day of the year. Morning star is in the New Testament's Book of Revelation identifying the Messiah: 'I am the sprig from the root of David and the bright star of the morning' (Revelation 22.16). 'Christ, that morning Star' is part of the Exultet read at the Easter Vigil.

The third and fourth lines are echoed by Zechariah, in what is called the Benedictus said daily at morning prayer, speaking after the birth of his son John the Baptist: '... to give light to those who live/in darkness and the shadow of dark as death' (Luke 1.79).

Augsburg Cathedral used to start the O Antiphons early on 13 December to allow for additions including O Thoma Didyme for St Thomas Day.

Old St Thomas's Day

Today used to be St Thomas's Day but in 1969 the Roman Catholic Church, followed by the Anglican Church in 1980, moved the feast day to 3 July which was the feast of the translation of his relics in 394. However, since 2000 the Anglican Church has made provision for a St Thomas celebration today for those wishing to maintain tradition. The day was associated with giving.

The appearance of Thomas in the Advent calendar was a reminder that Jesus whose birth is celebrated in four days' time suffered death and resurrection. Without this outcome Christmas would be of no importance and meaningless.

St Thomas

St Thomas is the Doubting Thomas Apostle who at the start of Holy Week offered to die with Jesus (John 11.16) and then refused to believe that Christ had risen after his death until he, Thomas himself, had touched the wounds (John 20.24-8).

According to strongly held local tradition, Thomas arrived in India in 52AD twenty years after Christ told his Apostles, just before the Ascension, that they would preach to 'all nations' (Matthew 28.19 and Luke 24.47). Thomas is believed to have travelled by way of Syria and Iran and to have met and baptised the Magi (see page 124) during the journey. He may have passed the next twenty years in Kerala before being martyred and buried in Mylapore. His tomb in the basilica is empty as his body was translated to Edessa in 394 and then to Chios in the Aegean in 1144. Since 1258 his remains have been in Ortona's St Thomas the Apostle Cathedral in Italy where the skull is carried in an outdoor procession in May. Meanwhile a skull kept at St John's monastery on the island of Patmos is also claimed as Thomas's. Mylapore, in its St Thomas Museum, has a bone described as a 'relic from the hand that touched the wound of Jesus Christ'. A finger is in Santa Croce in Gerusalemme in Rome.

St Thomas Becket (see page 96) was born today in 1118 and named after the saint. Following the adjustment to the calendar in the 18th century today is the shortest day of the year giving rise to the lines 'St Thomas gray, St Thomas gray,/The longest night and the shortest day'.

St Thomas's Day Traditions

St Thomas's Day was marked in many places by the custom of going A-Thomassing also known as Gooding – asking for presents to help in preparing for the Christmas feast – hence the rhyme 'St Thomas divine,/Brewing, baking and killing of fat swine'.

The poor went door to door asking for money, corn, meat or simply ingredients for the Christmas pudding (see page 12). The recipients, as a thank you for the dole, would sometimes give a sprig of holly in return. In some places money, maybe from a fund, was given out at the morning Mass in church.

In Warwickshire children would tour their village chanting the song:

> *Christmas is coming and the geese are getting fat,*
> *Please spare a penny for the old man's hat,*
> *If you haven't got a penny, a halfpenny will do,*
> *If you haven't got a halfpenny, God bless you.*

In the North Yorkshire Moors it was a tradition for boys to spend the day visiting farmhouses to ask for pepper cake or gingerbread and cheese.

In Radnorshire the chant was:

> *A-gooding*
> *A-gooding*
> *To make we a pudding.*

Here the tradition was for people to call at the big houses for a gift of wheat which millers ground free of charge.

In the Cotswolds it was the custom to collect apples and at Willersey, near Chipping Camden, the chant was:

> *Please to remember St Thomas's Day*
> *St Thomas's Day is the shortest day.*
> *Up the stocking and down the shoe,*
> *If you ain't got no apples, money'll do.*
> *Up the ladder and down the wall,*
> *A peck o' apples'll serve us all.*

In Brierley Hill, West Midlands, until the 1930s it was possible to have a visit from an old man who before holding out his cap would recite:

> *Please remember St Thomas' Day,*
> *The longest night and the shortest day.*
> *If you haven't got a penny, a ha'penny will do.*
> *If you haven't got a ha'penny, God bless you.*

Thomasing ended at Langley Marish in Buckinghamshire with Queen Victoria's reign. Days after the death in 1900 of lay rector John Nash, grandfather of war artist Paul, widows came for the last time on St Thomas's Day with baskets to collect a gift of wheat, oatmeal, corn and milk for Christmas.

The last record of Thomasing is at Hinton Martel in Dorset where the late Canon William Barnard kept the custom going until 1992. Here 5p coins (replacing the pre-decimal threepenny pieces) were distributed during this morning's Eucharist in accordance with the Dorset rhyme from when a threepence coin was offered door to door :

> *Go a-gooding*
> *And collect ingredients for the Christmas pudding.*

In Sweden this used to be the day to put up the Christmas pole (a slender spruce tree with just a few branches left near the top), a star or cross at the farm entrance to acknowledge the coming of Christmas.

As part of preparing for Christmas it was suggested in 1070 by the Archbishop Lanfranc of Canterbury that on St Thomas's Eve the faithful should take a bath — one of five he recommended per year.

In the Bible
John 20.24-8

Thomas was not in the Upper Room on Easter Day evening when Jesus appeared. The apostle was amazed and sceptical when the others told him what he had missed. He said: 'Unless I see the holes that the nails made in his hands and can put my finger into the holes they made, and unless I can put my hand into his side, I refuse to believe.' He was not convinced by his colleagues' claim until the following week when Jesus appeared again. Thomas was present and Christ invited him to put his hand into his side. 'My Lord and my God!' replied Thomas.

In Church
The O Oriens antiphon precedes the Gospel at Mass and bookends the Magnificat at evening prayer.

St Thomas's Day Events
In London the Clothworkers' Company has a St Thomas's Eve carol service on 20 December at St Olave's, Hart Street. This was the day on which the Company used to distribute money and make payments to poor clothworkers but since 1967 gifts of money have been made during the year according to need.

At Bilbao in Spain the St Thomas's Day Fair is a major event with around 250 stands selling local countryside products. Once Basque farmers would take their horse-drawn carts laden with produce to the town for Christmas shoppers. Other Basque Country towns and villages also have markets. Nearby San

Sebastian's Fiesta de Santo Tomás began in the 19th century when leaseholders of land came into the town to pay the annual rent and give landowners produce. Now farmers and craftspeople fill the streets of the old town to sell their sausages, cheeses, honey and cider. The day ends with an open-air dance. Some young people and children wear traditional costume.

Finnish capital Helsinki has a popular St Thomas Christmas Market which now opens at the beginning of Advent and ends tomorrow.

O Rex Gentium

22 December

Today's O Antiphon is O Rex Gentium.

> *O King of the nations, and their desire,*
> *the cornerstone making both one:*
> *Come and save the human race,*
> *which you fashioned from clay.*

(Common Worship)

> *'Now I shall lay a stone in Zion,*
> *a granite stone,*
> *a precious corner-stone,*
> *a firm foundation stone:*
> *no one who relies on this will stumble.'*

(Isaiah 28.16)

This is referred to by St Peter (1 Peter 2. 6) and alluded to by St Paul (Ephesians 2.20).

In Church

The O Rex Gentium antiphon precedes the Gospel at Mass and bookends the Magnificat at evening prayer.

O Emmanuel
23 December

O Emmanuel, our King and our lawgiver,
the hope of the nations and their Saviour:
Come and save us, O Lord our God.

(Common Worship)

'The Lord will give you a sign in any case:
It is this: the young woman is with child
and will give birth to a son
whom she will call Immanuel.'

(Isaiah 7.14)

Emmanuel, meaning God with us, is the name for the Messiah found in Isaiah where his birth is foretold and this is referred to at the beginning of St Matthew's Gospel (Matthew 1.23).

In Church
The O Emmanuel antiphon precedes the Gospel at Mass and the Magnificat at evening prayer.

CHRISTMAS

Christmas Eve

24 December

For many people, Christmas begins at 3pm when there is the hint of gathering darkness as the candlelit service of Nine Lessons and Carols is broadcast on BBC Radio 4 from King's College, Cambridge.

The Christmas tree is decorated today, cribs are blessed, children hang up a stocking when going to bed and people go to church just before midnight.

This coming night and tomorrow millions celebrate the birth, over 2,000 years ago, of the promised and longed for Messiah whose teaching guides them.

Cambridge Nine Lessons and Carols

The Service of Nine Lessons and Carols in the Chapel of Our Lady and St Nicholas at King's College, Cambridge has been broadcast by the BBC on radio since 1928. This was the year when the publication of *The Oxford Book of Carols* contributed to the growth of carol services elsewhere. The service was first held at King's in 1918 when the Dean of Chapel Eric Milner-White copied the Christmas Eve service held at Truro Cathedral.

The huge Cornish cathedral, which in the 1870s was still being built, incorporated as a chapel St Mary's Church whose choristers went out carol singing on Christmas Eve. In 1878, at the suggestion of Vicar Choral G.H.S. Walpole (later Bishop of Edinburgh) a late evening carol service was introduced on Christmas Eve as a rival attraction to drinking in Truro's pubs.

Bishop of Truro Edward Benson turned this service into the Nine Lessons with Carols which he devised, according to his son, using 'ancient sources'. This probably included the Sarum rite Christmas matins which had nine readings and the O Antiphons which were each read or intoned by a different person.

The first service in 1880 began at 10pm and Bishop Benson read the ninth and final lesson himself. Due to construction work this gathering was in a wooden building on the site of today's cathedral restaurant called, appropriately, Benson's. In 1883 he became Archbishop of Canterbury, which led to St Mary Lambeth, at the Lambeth Palace gate, introducing the service at 8pm on Christmas Eve with choristers reading all nine lessons. The Archbishop also had an official residence at Addington in Surrey where from 1884 St Mary's held the service at 3pm on the Sunday after Christmas Day. *Nine Lessons and Carols: A Festal Service for Christmastide* was published the same year but as late as 1902 the parish was promoting the service as carols 'sung in accordance with the Addington use'. A decade earlier the rector had written: 'We know of no carol service which can compare with it for effect and variety'. With the St Mary Lambeth building having closed in 1972, and become the Garden Museum, Addington's church now claims in its carol service sheet that it is 'believed to be the first parish church to use this carol service'.

At Cambridge the bidding prayer still has traces of its origins in the First World War by remembering 'those who rejoice with us, but upon another shore and in a greater light'. The service, broadcast worldwide, begins when a young chorister, chosen moments earlier, stands at the west end of the 289 foot long chapel and sings solo the first verse of *Once in Royal David's city*. This has been the opening processional hymn since 1919 but the custom predates King's adopting the service for as early as 1912 it was already the tradition for its choir to gather at the west end just before 5pm on Christmas Eve and sing the first verse of Once in Royal David's City. Others took up the second verse as the choristers moved east. Today people queue from early morning for a seat and for many in America the broadcast is part of Christmas Eve breakfast. Truro now holds the service at 7pm.

Midnight Mass

By tradition Christ was born on the stroke of midnight. The first midnight Mass was in Bethlehem around 400 and later that century the Pope began the custom of celebrating Mass at midnight in Santa Maria Maggiore which displays parts of the original crib.

Although the habit of midnight Mass grew in the British Isles during the last half of the 20th century in Anglican churches and even Methodist churches, there is now another change discernible. A significant and growing number of churches in recent years have begun the Midnight Mass at 11.30pm or had carols sung up to midnight before starting the Mass. The tradition of arriving for a service beginning at midnight has almost disappeared.

With the introduction of the anticipated Sunday Mass (Mass on Saturday night for Sunday), many people now go to Christmas Mass well before midnight. Westminster Cathedral's Vigil Sung Mass on Christmas Eve is not only packed but is the Christmas Mass for those present with darkness having fallen and the final candle on the Advent Wreath lit. Dublin's Pro-Cathedral replaced Midnight Mass with a Mass of Christmas Night at 10pm some years before St Peter's Rome moved its midnight celebration forward by two hours coinciding with midnight in Bethlehem. Now the Vatican begins even earlier at 9.30pm. At Brighton's Chapel Royal, the 8pm 'midnight Mass' has now moved to 5.30pm resulting in a very full church.

The new trend, 'Mass during the night' rather than 'midnight Mass', is probably inevitable but it does still preserve elements of the early church meeting at night and singing psalms whilst waiting for the celebration hour.

The Crib

In very early times the Christmas Mass was celebrated with a representation of the crib into which the host was placed. The first Crib scene was erected around 432 in Rome's Santa Maria Maggiore. The version with live animals was prepared by St

Francis of Assisi in 1223 inside a cave at Greccio near Assisi just three years after he had visited Bethlehem.

Now model cribs, reflecting regional influences and sometimes lavish, are found all over the world. Enriching the scene with a local or contemporary element makes it not only a commemoration but an immediate event.

As recently as 1953 Pius XII, unhappy about the spread of the Christmas Tree custom, encouraged cribs. In 2002 Norwich Cathedral had a crib with live sheep and geese. The inclusion of the ox and donkey started by St Francis is derived not from a New Testament account but from Isaiah 1.3: 'The ox knows its owner and the donkey its master's crib.'

The crib remains in church, and in Rome's St Peter's Square, until 2 February (see page 155).

What happened today

There were many witnesses to Jesus' crucifixion unlike his birth which was a quiet unrecorded event. The belief in Jesus being born at Bethlehem rests solely with the account given in St Luke's Gospel.

Why Mary and Joseph should leave Nazareth and go to Bethlehem so late in the pregnancy is a mystery as the date of the census requirement does not coincide with Jesus' birth and neither parent was a Roman citizen. But this was the reason given by Luke who had learnt about Jesus' early life from the Apostles and read St Matthew's Gospel which includes the passage from Micah (5.1-3) written 700 years earlier: 'Bethlehem...from will come for me a future ruler of Israel.' It may be that the census took place over several years and Joseph was required in Bethlehem as part-owner of family property.

If Luke is correct then Jesus was born late at night in overcrowded Bethlehem accommodation and laid in a manger in the stable. Mary and Joseph may have been staying at a family home or an inn.

Meanwhile, news of the event is said to have been relayed by angels to shepherds, on night-watch in fields down the hill from the small town, who resolved to visit the Holy Family (Luke 2.1-15). Only they had an inkling of the significance of the birth. The stable was probably the cave which is now preserved under the Church of the Nativity. In Hebrew, *Bethlehem* means *house of bread* (as does *Bethany* where Jesus stayed during the last week of his ministry).

In Church

'Midnight Mass' (see above) is the main service with carols (Appendix page 165). The liturgical colour for vestments is white. Either at the beginning or end the Christ Child baby figure is carried to the Crib which is then blessed and censed. The other crib figures, in addition to Mary and Joseph and maybe some cattle, might include the shepherds but not the Three Kings who do not arrive until 6 January (see page 122). The Kings can be placed elsewhere in the church and day by day moved closer to the crib to symbolise their journey.

After the four weeks of Advent, the Gloria is heard again. The first verse ('Glory to God in the highest, and on earth peace to people of good will') is the angels' hymn which according to St Luke was heard by the shepherds during the night that Jesus was born.

It is the custom tonight to kneel briefly during the Creed at the words 'and by the Holy Spirit was incarnate of the Virgin Mary, and became man'.

Suitable carols (see page 165) are *Once in royal David's city* (often sung at the start); *Silent night, holy night* which was written specially for midnight Mass and *O come all ye faithful* which has a special Christmas Day verse at the end.

In Bethlehem Tonight

At the end of Midnight Mass in Bethlehem's Church of the Nativity it is the custom for the Latin Patriarch of Jerusalem to carry the Christ Child image down into the Holy Grotto where Christ is believed to have been born.

At Greccio in Italy Tonight

The first live crib scene is recreated by young people late this evening. This is repeated during the twelve days of Christmas and on Epiphany afternoon.

Other Events

An old Irish tradition of putting a candle in the front window to welcome the Holy Family is observed in some Dublin homes. Residents of Campden Hill Square in London have maintained the custom since 1926. Pope Benedict XVI put a candle in his window above St Peter's Square.

At Exeter Cathedral there is at 6pm the ancient Office of Bishop John Grandisson for Christmas Eve involving choristers with lighted tapers emerging from behind the high altar to announce in Latin, first in the Quire and then the nave, the birth of Christ. This was part of the Christmas Eve vespers from at least 1369 and now forms the opening of the carol service. 'At the beginning the choir sings, distant and ethereal, illuminated by a few candles, lost in the surrounding darkness,' wrote Simon Hoggart who witnessed it in 2002. The cathedral introduced Midnight Mass only in 2015.

At Dewsbury Minster in Yorkshire, beginning at about 10.15pm, the Black Tom tenor bell is tolled for every year since Christ's birth – now over 2000 times – and the last ring coincides with midnight. The tolling can be heard during the First Communion of Christmas which begins at 11.15pm. This custom, begun in 1434 and revived in 1828, is known as 'tolling of the devil's knell' as it is said to have been started to remind the devil of his defeat. Three bell ringers take turns with ringing the Black Tom bell whilst another person marks off the years to ensure the correct number of rings. The custom was featured on one of the 1986 Christmas stamps.

Traditions

Christmas Tree

The Christmas tree is said to have been invented in 723 by St Boniface when he dramatically felled the pagan Oak of Thor at Geismar in Germany and claimed a fir growing in the oak's roots as the new symbol. The evergreen fir is a sign of life that does not die even in winter. Crediton in Devon, where Boniface was born, has an annual Christmas Tree Festival in its parish church.

John Stow claimed that a tree had been put up in Cornhill in the City of London in 1444. But Sélestat in the French region of Alsace claims to have introduced the Christmas tree in 1531 with undecorated fir trees taken indoors.

The first record of a decorated tree is at Riga in Latvia in 1510 which is around the time Martin Luther is credited with introducing candles on the branches. Christmas trees were in Strasbourg by at least 1605. But the Christmas tree custom only arrived in Boniface's home country in the 18th century through George III's German wife Charlotte who arranged for one lit with candles at Kew Palace in the 1790s. Queen Adelaide had a tree at Brighton Pavilion in the 1830s, about the time German merchants introduced them to Manchester. But it was Queen Victoria's 1848 tree at Windsor Castle, depicted in *The Illustrated London News* and described in *The Times*, which was copied by English families. Today the Queen gives trees from Windsor Great Park to St Paul's Cathedral. A tree from Balmoral is sent to Canongate Kirk in Edinburgh. The tradition of placing a Christmas tree in Rome's St Peter's Square began only in 1982.

In Germany and Poland the tree is decorated today.

Stocking

This evening's custom of children hanging up a stocking to be filled with presents by Father Christmas, first found early in the 19th century in parts of England and Germany, is derived from the story of St Nicholas (see page 27).

Christmas Day
25 December

About 204 Hippolytus of Rome, in his commentary on the Book of Daniel, claimed that Jesus was born on 25 December and this date was adopted as Christmas Day in northern Italy, Spain and Antioch. Pope Julius I (337-352) is credited with confirming the universal date. Christmas coincided with a recently introduced Roman festival Natalis Solis Invicti ('birth of the unconquered sun'), recognising the lengthening days, and so the seasonal greeting in Italy remains Buon Natale. The English word 'Christmas' comes from the Saxon *Cristes Maesse* meaning 'Mass of Christ' first recorded in 1038.

The year of Christ's birth is now thought to be around 6BC.

What Happened Today
Luke 2.16-20
The shepherds (alerted during the night by the angels or maybe messengers since the word is *angelos* in Greek) found Mary and Joseph with newly-born Jesus at lodgings in Bethlehem. They left rejoicing and glorifying God for the great event.

Relics
Santa Maria Maggiore in Rome displays in the open crypt before the high altar what are said to be five wooden slats of the crib in which Jesus was laid. The relics were brought from the Holy Land in 642 and given to the church which was for a time called St Mary of the Crib. The basilica also has the oldest nativity scene figures, about three foot high, which date from around 1290. According to tradition the church is built in the place where the

Virgin told Pope Liberius in a dream that snow would fall on 5 August 358. The church was completed a century later by Pope Sixtus III following the Council of Ephesus which declared Mary to be the Mother of God. The miracle is recalled every 5 August with a shower of white jasmine petals from the basilica's ceiling above the altar during the singing of the Gloria at Mass and the Magnificat at Vespers.

The tunic of the Blessed Virgin Mary, known as the Sancta Camisia and said to have been worn by her in Bethlehem, has been in the care of Chartres Cathedral since 876.

Aachen Cathedral has a golden chest in the sanctuary holding the what is claimed as the Christ Child's swaddling clothes and his mother's dress. (Also in the reliquary are the alleged cloth which was wrapped around John the Baptist's decapitated head and the loin cloth worn by Christ on the cross.) The Christmas Mass is celebrated in front of these relics which have been at Aachen since 1239 and are only exposed briefly every seven years (2021/2028/2035).

In Church

Today there is normally a Mass of the Dawn at 8am or 9am. Later in the morning there is the main Mass of Christmas although for many the midnight celebration will have been the main climax to Advent. Today's vestments are white as at the vigil and Midnight Mass. As last night it is the custom today to kneel briefly during the Creed at the mention of the incarnation.

Other Early Hour Christmas Day Services

In Wales pre-dawn was the traditional time for the Plygain service until the end of the 19th century. *Plygain*, derived from *pulli canto* meaning cock crow and pronounced 'plugine', incorporates matins and can begin as early as 3am and last until daylight as many of the sixty Welsh carols are sung. It evolved in the 16th century after the midnight and dawn Masses were abolished at the Reformation. Most churches started at 6am and ended at about 8am with, in later years, sometimes a restored dawn celebration of the Eucharist. Originally only males were present at the early hour. The informal service, often by candlelight, survives in only a very few places on Christmas Day. The remote Hen Bethel Chapel on the Black Mountain was reached by worshippers walking a mile in the dark with torches. At St John's in Carmarthen the tradition of a 6am 'Y Plygain', a Mass in Welsh, lasted until the close of the 20th century.

But Plygain survives in some places as a Christmas Eve service sometimes starting at 11pm and so maybe returning now to its roots in a pre-Reformation Midnight Mass. It is also maintained on the Sunday after Christmas Day, especially in the valley churches around Llanfihangel yng Ngwynfa, as an early evening carol service, with sometimes readings and poems replacing matins. The emphasis is at all times on the traditional and often haunting Welsh carols with harp accompaniment. The carols have at least twenty verses and feature not only Christ's birth but his life, death and resurrection. Plygain was portrayed with three women in tall hats bearing candles on one of the 1986 Christmas stamps.

In Sweden an early morning Lutheran church service called Julotta takes place at 7 or 8am during which the building slowly fills with light as a flame is passed from person to person lighting each individual's candle.

Christmas Feasting

The turkey was introduced from America by, allegedly, the strongly Protestant William Strickland who gave one to Elizabeth I. His parish church at Boynton in Yorkshire has a lectern featuring a turkey rather than the traditional eagle. Today traditional lunch includes the pudding which may have been made on Christ The King Sunday. Mince pies lost their original oblong crib shape by the 1690s and the meat was replaced by today's sweet spiced version in the 1860s.

The Queen's Broadcast

In the United Kingdom and Commonwealth, the Queen's broadcast in the afternoon follows a tradition begun in 1932 when George V spoke live on radio to the Empire. The message has been televised since 1957 but ceased to be live in 1960. The pre-recording enabled the message to be shown simultaneously round the Commonwealth and, although satellites now allow for world-wide live broadcasting, the recording continues to be made about five days before transmission. The only gaps in the annual custom have been in 1936, 1938 and 1969. Being a message to the Commonwealth, the Queen does not speak on the advice of her UK ministers but personally and usually ends by emphasising her Christian faith. In 2006 Her Majesty recorded the broadcast in Southwark Cathedral.

Boxing Day

St Stephen's Day

26 December

On this day, the second of the Twelve Days of Christmas, there is an immediate reminder that the consequence of yesterday's birth is that Christ was persecuted and killed as are many of his followers. This is the possible cost of the faith proclaimed yesterday.

Today Stephen, the first Christian martyr, is remembered. He, like Christ, asked for his murderers to be forgiven. In the play *Murder in the Cathedral*, T. S. Eliot has Thomas Becket say: 'Is it an accident, do you think, that the day of the first martyr follows immediately the day of the Birth of Christ? By no means.'

The Council of Tours in 567 declared that the days between Christmas Day and Epiphany (6 January) should be a holiday and in modern times this has again become a custom for many. Today has been a Bank Holiday in the British Isles since 1871 except in Scotland where it has only been day off work since 1974. (Scotland did not have a holiday on Christmas Day until 1958 although it has always been a common law holiday in England.) The public holiday is called 'Bank' because bills due on the day off are payable the next day. However, in the 1990s some DIY shops started opening for sales on Boxing Day and since 2003 it has become a massive shopping day with sale launches at chain stores.

During the next eight days, the Octave of Christmas, the special days continue to highlight the implications of Christ's birth.

St Stephen

Stephen, a Greek-speaking Jew, died about two years after Christ's crucifixion. The well-read deacon was a zealous preacher in Jerusalem and this led to an appearance before the Sanhedrin, the Jewish council with civil authority. He boldly denounced it as 'stiff-necked' and accused members of persecuting and killing Christ.

They responded by taking Stephen outside the city wall, probably through the Damascus Gate, and stoning him to death. Watching and approving was Saul who later converted and who we now know as St Paul.

Stephen's remains were found outside Jerusalem in 415 and for a time were in Constantinople before being brought to Rome by Pope Pelagius in about 579. He had them placed alongside St Lawrence, another famous deacon, in San Lorenzo Fuori le Mura (St Lawrence outside the Walls), one of the Seven Pilgrim Churches of Rome. Their lives are depicted in 13th-century frescoes in the portico whilst their relics are behind a grille in the crypt below the high altar.

Stephen is patron of altar servers, coffin makers, deacons and the Palace of Westminster. Its Chapel of St Stephen saw the feast day observed from 1348 to 1547 after which it became the Commons chamber. In its last years as a chapel, the setting of the Mass would have been written by the chapel's composer and verger Nicholas Ludford.

In 1977 Cardinal Basil Hume of Westminster dedicated CAFOD (Catholic Fund for Overseas Development) to St Stephen as his job was to help the poor and widowed receive a fair share of the early Christian community's wealth.

Boxing Day

In 1606 Shakespeare's *King Lear* had its première before James I 'at Whitehall upon St Stephen's night in Christmas holidays'. Later the name Boxing Day came into use due to the collecting box carried around house to house by boys and the custom of opening the church poor box and distributing the contents today.

In the 1660s Samuel Pepys gave 'boxes' (money and presents) to tradesmen today and so did Parson Woodforde at Weston Longville in Norfolk just over a century later. By the late 19th century it became customary for tradesmen to call today and receive a few coins or even a note. In the second half of the 20th century tips were still given to dustmen and milkmen just before Christmas but now the idea of a 'Christmas Box', or seasonal tip, has disappeared with rising wages.

Abroad it is only at Palermo in Sicily that today is also known as Boxing Day. Boxes of food, money and gifts are collected and given to the needy and various charitable institutions. Local bands play and food vendors appear.

In The Bible
Acts 6 and 7
Stephen stands up to his accusers and is executed.

In Church
Churches dedicated to St Stephen often observe the day with as much ceremony and attendance as Christmas Day. The colour of vestments switches from white to red for a martyr.

The readings include the account of Stephen's death in the Acts of the Apostles.

Today has its own carol *Good King Wenceslas*. The so-called king is St Wenceslas, born in 907, who was Duke of Bohemia from about 925 under Charlemagne's successor King Henry. Wenceslaus' grandfather had been converted to Christianity by St Cyril and St Methodius. Wenceslas set about encouraging Christianity and building churches but was eventually murdered by his brother in 935. Bohemia is now the Czech Republic where Wenceslas is the patron saint with his equestrian statue dominating Prague's Wenceslas Square. This was a focus for demonstrations before the fall of communism. His tomb is in nearby St Vitus Cathedral where he is honoured on St Wenceslaus' Day, his martyrdom anniversary, 28 September. The carol was written about 1850 by priest and hymn writer J. M. Neale who encouraged carol singing in East Grinstead's High Street. The snow and winter fuel references, although based on an incident in the saint's life, were inspired by the snowy view of Ashdown Forest seen from Neale's study at Sackville College on the edge of the small town. The imagery suggests that we should walk in Christ's footsteps. The reference to St Agnes's Well may be associated with Neale's daughter Agnes. He included St Agnes of Rome among four women saints depicted in the chapel and built a St Agnes well in the college quadrangle. The tune comes from a 13th-century spring song.

If today is a Sunday then St Stephen's Day gives way to The Holy Family (see page 109) although churches dedicated to Stephen often keep their patronal festival as usual.

Today at St Stephen's tomb

At San Lorenzo fuori le Mura in Rome there is 8am Mass and Solemn Mass at 6.30pm.

Boxing Day Events

The Pope leads The Angelus from his window above St Peter's Square at noon. 'The martyrs of today are greater in number than those of the first centuries,' said Pope Francis today in 2016.

The white Christmas candles on the window ledges at St Stephen's Church in Bournemouth are replaced by red for the morning Solemn Mass. The pine cone Christmas decorations are a reminder of the pine logs featured in *Good King Wenceslas* which is sung as the offertory hymn. Afterwards the congregation enjoys mince pies and drinks. Similar services can be found at London's St Stephen's Gloucester Road, St Stephen's Rochester Row, St Stephen's-on-the-Cliffs in Blackpool and also at the Brisbane and Vienna cathedrals which are both dedicated to Stephen. In Vienna the cathedral's Pummerin bell, rung only on special occasions, can be heard across the city shortly before midday as the main morning Mass ends.

In Ireland today is known only as St Stephen's Day. In the morning young boys and men dress up as Wren Boys and walk around, sometimes also singing hymns, knocking at doors to raise money for charity. They either blacken their faces, to recall chimney sweeps once involved in the custom, or wear straw costumes similar to those associated with Plough Monday in East Anglia (see page 134). This mainly rural Irish custom once involved killing a wren because the bird was said to have betrayed Stephen's hiding place by chattering. The custom used to take place elsewhere in the British Isles including Wales, on Twelfth Night, and in Oxfordshire. There is an English connection in Ireland today with St George featuring as a character in Dingle. The Wren Boy custom has returned not only in Ireland but to the Isle of Man where it mainly involves much country dancing in the streets before midday. The Irish revival, after a sixty year gap, began gradually in the 1980s in Dublin's Sandymount Green where as many as a thousand join in a mid-morning festival of mummers involving a song, dance and collecting for charity by asking for 'a penny for the wren' at pubs and houses. The custom is observed on Monday when 26 December falls on Holy Family Sunday.

At Marshfield in Wiltshire, carols announced by the vicar are sung from 10.30am in the Market Place. At 11am seven mummers dressed in costumes made from strips of newspaper and coloured paper, and led by the town crier with his handbell, arrive. They perform a five minute long play featuring St George and Old Father Christmas. It is repeated at the top of Sheepfair Lane, the top of St Martins's Lane, the Almshouses and outside one of the three pubs. The Marshfield play, which may date from 1141, was discontinued in the 1880s when a number of the players died of influenza but in 1931 it was revived after the vicar heard his gardener reciting part of the play. All players are males from local families and must have a local accent.

At Crookham in Hampshire, a mumming play featuring a doctor in a top hat and Father Christmas, is performed outside the George and Lobster, the Black Horse, the Queen's Head and on the Crescent Green. The custom began here in the 1850s.

The Gloucester Mummers Play, revived in 1969, is

performed outside the cathedral at noon followed by Morris dancing. Laurie Lee was the Gloucester mummers patron.

The Keynsham Mummers Play, which has been performed at least since 1822 and revived in 1976, is staged at noon by the Bristol Morris Men at Keysham's New Inn following a performance outside the parish church. As the script is incomplete, performances differ slightly but include a rendering of Good King Wenceslas.

At Greatham, near Hartlepool, the Greatham Sword Dance, the last authentic sword dance with a real long sword which was revived in 1967, and a mummers play are performed at noon outside the Hospital of God gates in Front Street.

In Ripon the Sword Dance play, a short mumming play which does not involve a sword, is performed by three people many times around the town. Meanwhile the Bishop of Ripon and Leeds celebrates the Eucharist in the cathedral this morning before leading a pilgrimage to Fountains Abbey. The four mile walk commemorates the journey in 1132 by thirteen Benedictine monks who, on their way from York, stopped at the cathedral for Christmas lunch before finding the site for the future abbey the following day. The annual walk has been held since 1982 when 132 people joined in. Now there are around 2,000. Pilgrims are fortified with mulled wine and mince pies at the Abbey entrance where those unable to walk swell the numbers. A short service with carols and a brass band is held in the vaulted cellarium among the ruins at noon before the return trek. 'The walk represents our commitment to following in Christ's way throughout the coming year', said Bishop Richard Packer in 2003.

St John's Day

27 December

St John the Evangelist was an Apostle but his life is also a reminder, after yesterday, that not all followers have to die for the faith.

St John

John was a fisherman and with his brother James, who is remembered in a few days' time (see page 98), was called by Jesus to be a disciple and one of the twelve Apostles. John is sometimes known as 'John the Divine' because he became a theologian and this is reflected in St John's Gospel which he may have written. Certainly he and his brother were with Christ at such crucial moments as the Transfiguration and the vigil in the Garden of Gethsemane. John reached the empty tomb of Christ first after the resurrection.

Later he was exiled to the Greek island of Patmos and is believed to have died in AD 100 at the age of about 90 in Ephesus (now part of Turkey) where he had cared for the Virgin Mary as instructed by Jesus from the Cross.

John was buried at nearby Selçuk where a church, now a ruin, was erected over the site in the mid-6th century by Emperor Justinian. John, also called the 'Disciple that Jesus loved', is a familiar figure depicted on many church rood screens with the Virgin Mary.

He is patron of theologians, authors, love, loyalty and friendship.

In The Bible

St Mark 1.16-20 and St Luke 5.10

Holy Innocents

28 December

Today is an out of sequence commemoration of the murder of babies by King Herod of Judea who saw the birth of Christ as a threat. The Wise Men, or Three Kings, were aware of Herod's fear of a rival king in his country and did not reveal the whereabouts of Baby Jesus.

Herod, although not a Jew, was given the title King of the Jews by the Romans. The terrible incident and the Holy Family's escape to safety in Egypt may have taken place some months, or even two years, after Christ's birth. This was a desperate move as Jews would have been horrified at having to go to Egypt but the result may be that Jesus spent some of his early childhood there until the death of deranged Herod at the age of 68.

It has been suggested that these children should be called 'the first Christian martyrs'. Stephen (see page 89), who is called 'the first Christian martyr', knowingly risked his life for the faith about thirty-five years later.

Westminster Abbey, built by St Edward the Confessor, was consecrated on Holy Innocents 1065. St Paul's-Outside-the-Walls in Rome has a mosaic depicting the Cross with five of the Holy Innocents underneath.

Childermas

Pre-Reformation, muffled bells were rung and black vestments worn at Mass today. But today was also known as Childermas as it was a choristers' day and the final day of the reign of the boy bishop elected on St Nicholas Day (see page 27). Boys sang the divine office whilst clergy would act as servers and carry candles although one priest remained in role to celebrate the Mass. The cathedrals in Burgos and Palencia today install a boy bishop who rides through the streets on a white horse.

In England as late as 1594 it was still a day of fun with a lord of misrule presiding over revels at Gray's Inn hall when Shakespeare's *The Comedy of Errors* was first performed.

In Spain, Latin America and the Philippines this remains a day for fun and jokes including spoof stories in newspapers. The excuse for this is that Mary may have had to trick Herod's soldiers to pass through the checkpoint on her way to Egypt.

The commemoration has been observed at this time separate from The Epiphany since about 485.

Murder of the Innocents

Matthew 2. 16-18

Herod, who is said to have ordered the death of all children aged 2 years or under in and around Bethlehem, is known to have murdered his own sons. Indeed the occasional mass murder during his rule was not unknown. Being a small village it has been thought that Herod's order probably resulted in the death of about seven babies and at most 25 infants. However, the Cave of the Holy Innocents, next to the Church of the Nativity, contains a large number of bones. In recounting the story, Matthew would have been aware of the passage in Exodus (2.1-10) about Moses being hidden during the massacre of male babies.

Flight into Egypt

Matthew 2: 13-15

According to tradition the Holy Family travelled by way of Medinat and Farma in northern Sinai to Assiut in Upper Egypt. At Matariya, on the edge of Cairo, there is the Virgin Mary sycamore tree under which they are said to have rested. Their arrival is said to have caused a spring to appear. Here it is believed that Mary washed clothes in the stream and Joseph worked on a building site for several months. A child's footprint in stone is kept in a cupboard at the back of the church.

In Old Cairo there is the Church of St Sergius built over a cave where the Holy Family is said to have found refuge on 1 June.

Mostorod, a village near Cairo, is claimed to have been home to the Holy Family for two weeks in August. In the capital's suburb of Maadi, meaning crossing, the Christ Child and his parents are thought to have crossed the Nile or boarded a boat back to Upper Egypt.

A small church near Kafr al-Sheikh, in the Nile Delta, also has a footprint in stone said to have been made by the infant Jesus.

On Herod's death his kingdom was divided by the Romans into three areas and Mary and Joseph were directed by an angel to live in their home town of Nazareth where the ruler was potentially less severe than in the Bethlehem area. In Egypt the period of the Holy Family's stay is given as four years although it may have been just two.

In Church

The Old Testament reference to 'Rachel weeping for her children' in the gospel reading (Matthew 2.13-18) may have been inspired by Matthew knowing that Rachel's Tomb was near Bethlehem. The first reading today can be Jeremiah 31.15-17 which includes the passage.

Prayers are often said today for unintended martyrs.

A suitable carol is *Lully, lulla, thou little tiny child*, which is a 15th-century song once sung in Coventry during Corpus Christi street theatre depicting the slaughter.

Vestments are red for martyrs.

Today in Bethlehem

Mass is celebrated this morning in the tiny St Joseph's Chapel in the Cave of the Holy Innocents. Vespers, again attended by only a few in the confined space, follows in the afternoon.

St Thomas of Canterbury's Day

29 December

Today provides another reminder of the cost of following the Baby born in a manger. On the fifth day of Christmas 1170 the Archbishop of Canterbury Thomas Becket was murdered in his cathedral for putting God's law before the state.

St Thomas of Canterbury appointed Archbishop

Thomas Becket was Chancellor of England until 1162 when Henry II made him Archbishop of Canterbury hoping he would be an ally. Reluctant Becket was ordained priest the day before being consecrated bishop. To the King's surprise Becket gave his loyalty to the Church and resisted secular interference. He defended ecclesiastical courts and clashed with the King over church appointments. Eventually the tension between King and Primate was so bad that the Archbishop went abroad.

Last Days

Becket returned home just after Advent Sunday 1170 for what turned out to be the last few weeks of his life.

Having sailed from Wissant near Calais on Tuesday 1 December, the Archbishop arrived in Canterbury on Wednesday 2 December. About a week later, probably Friday 11 December, he rode to Southwark Priory (now the Cathedral) in London where the canons came out to welcome him.

He stayed the night next door at the Bishop of Winchester's palace where in the morning he discovered that he was being barred by Royal command from entering towns. He had upset the King's son Henry by suspending the Archbishop of York and excommunicating the Bishops of London and Salisbury for taking part without his permission in a coronation of the Henry as Regent to rule in his father's absence in France.

The Archbishop went north to his manor house at Harrow to try and make contact with Regent Henry who was thought to be at Woodstock. However, he was at Fordingbridge in Hampshire and so on Thursday 17 December, Becket, having celebrated Mass and preached at St Mary's, Harrow on the Hill, returned to Canterbury for the fourth Sunday in Advent and his birthday on St Thomas's Day Monday 21 December.

On Christmas Day Becket preached in the Cathedral on the theme 'peace on earth to men of goodwill' but felt obliged to announce the excommunications of those who held church office without authority and, in one case, had cut off the tail of a horse during the archbishop's visit to Harrow and stolen his wine. The primate recalled his martyred predecessor Alphege and suggested that there might soon be another. The congregation was appalled.

Meanwhile the King was in France raging against the Archbishop for questioning the crowning of his son and insisting on making his own church appointments. The famous line attributed to Henry, 'Will no one rid me of this troublesome priest?', is not found in any records but the King did commission three barons to cross the Channel and arrest Becket. However they were overtaken by four knights who set out to murder the Archbishop.

What Happened on Tuesday 29 December 1170

The four knights enjoyed a long lunch with much wine at St Augustine's Abbey in Canterbury. At about 3pm they arrived at the Archbishop's Palace by way of the gateway opposite St Alphege Lane in Palace Street.

The household was finishing lunch in the palace's hall decorated for Christmas with evergreen branches. An already apprehensive Archbishop had just eaten pheasant commenting that it was proper for any man about to go to his God to appear happy. Earlier in the day he had made his confession to his chaplain. The unwelcome and slightly drunk visitors confronted Becket in his first floor bedroom which was just to the right of today's main Old Palace gateway. The site is now a garden outside the present Archbishop's dining room. After a long heated debate the four went outside into the yard where they struggled into their armour.

The Archbishop was persuaded to go into the cathedral by way of a little used tunnel leading into the cellarer's hall. A door on the far side opened into the west walk of the cloister. This door may have been in the bay to the left of today's Michael Ramsey plaque. Archbishop Becket, led by a priest carrying the primatial cross, turned right and left to pass along the south walk. Two people ran ahead to warn that the Archbishop was in danger. It was getting dark and Vespers was already being sung in the choir.

Becket had just entered the north transept door when the now armed knights caught up. Monks poured out of their stalls but Becket, refusing to run and hide or have the cathedral doors locked, was hit on the back with a sword and had his skull cap flicked off. 'I am ready to give my life for the freedom of the Holy Church, in the name of him who purchased her peace in His blood,' said Becket calmly. The confrontation was drawn out since the knights had not intended the killing to take place in the cathedral. But Becket, who would not be dragged outside, was eventually felled. An accomplice of the murderers stepped forward with a sword to jerk the brains on to the stone floor shouting 'Come along! He'll never get up again'. A visitor who saw the incident recalled that the Archbishop met his death with 'his neck bent as if he were in prayer'.

Afterwards

Europe was deeply shocked as the news spread. The King heard about the murder on Friday 1 January and by February the Pope was informed. Meanwhile the cathedral remained closed. The Archbishop was first buried in the crypt which reopened to the public in April 1171. The rest of the cathedral opened almost a year afterwards on St Thomas's Day 21 December.

On Ash Wednesday 1173 Becket was canonised and the following year the King came to do penance at Canterbury by walking barefoot from St Dunstan's outside the city and kneeling all night at the tomb. Southwark Priory rededicated its existing sanatorium to the new saint – hence today's St Thomas' Hospital. The fresco of the murder in St John and St Paul at Spoleto in Italy dates from this time.

By 1174 a chapel had been dedicated to Thomas in Toledo Cathedral. In Salamanca in 1175 the first church was dedicated to Thomas Becket. That year Henry returned to Canterbury on Maundy Thursday and placed on Becket's tomb a charter granting privileges to the cathedral. On the 7 July 1220 the body was moved upstairs to the Trinity Chapel where for over 300 years, until Henry VIII ordered its destruction in 1538, it was one of Europe's greatest shrines.

The first church in England dedicated to Becket was begun in 1173 to stand alongside the entrance to Peterborough Abbey (now Cathedral). It was opened in 1177 by the new abbot Benedict who, as Prior of Canterbury, had been within earshot of Becket's murder. He wrote the first account of the incident and brought the martyr's shirt, two phials of his blood and a blood-stained flagstone on which Becket had fallen. The chapel nave site is now occupied by a branch of a coffee house chain, whilst the chancel, rebuilt in 1320, is the cathedral tearoom.

In 1176 a St Thomas Chapel had been opened in Lyon (where Becket was in exile) and another built on London Bridge. A few miles downstream the new Lesnes Abbey was in 1178 dedicated to the saint. Next year a mosque in Catania in Sicily was turned into a church dedicated to Thomas. In 1188 a chapel (now the Anglican cathedral) was dedicated to Thomas at Portsmouth and the refounded Waltham Abbey had a St Thomas infirmary chapel added.

Margaret of France, Henry II's widow, became Queen of Hungary and between 1186 and her death in 1197 she built a chapel to Thomas on St Thomas Hill opposite the cathedral at

Esztergom. Englishman Robertus Anglicus was archbishop and together they promoted the Thomas Becket cult.

In 1225 the new church at Chapel-en-le-Frith in Derbyshire was dedicated to St Thomas Becket. On 29 December 1226 Brunswick Cathedral in Germany was dedicated to three saints including Thomas due to the earlier influence of Henry's eldest daughter Matilda.

Later Marsala Cathedral in Sicily was also given the dedication after Henry II's youngest daughter Joan married the King of Sicily in 1177. By this time the dowager Queen Margaret of Sicily already had a Becket pendant containing a scrap of blood stained material. She is buried in Monreale Cathedral where the apse completed by 1189 has a mosaic of Becket.

More than a century later, in London, brewers formed the Guild of Our Lady and St Thomas Becket (now the Brewers' Company). It is suggested that the dedication was partly due to pilgrims drinking ale on their way from London to Becket's shrine at Canterbury. Geoffrey Chaucer's *The Canterbury Tales*, written in the late 14th century, is set on the pilgrimage route.

Canterbury's Roman Catholic Church of St Thomas has a statue of St Thomas More who was executed on 6 July 1535, the Eve of the Translation of St Thomas (7 July). More's head is buried in Canterbury's St Dunstan's Church. As More faced death in London for defying Henry VIII he said: 'I am a loyal servant of the King but God's servant first.' Becket had also died for the primacy of the Church and its faith in Christ.

St Thomas Becket's martyrdom has been compared to the death of Christ. Becket was aware that he might be having to suffer like Christ. When the Archbishop arrived back from exile on 2 December, to ride through villages to Canterbury, clothes were laid on the ground and there were shouts of 'Blessed is he that cometh in the name of the Lord'. Finally he entered a Canterbury gateway to a tumultuous welcome. This was his 'Palm Sunday' for like Christ entering Jerusalem he was received in triumph. On his last night the Archbishop looked out of the bedroom window contemplating fleeing to

Sandwich where there would be a safe ship to France. This was his 'Garden of Gethsemane' moment. The debate with the knights in the Palace was his 'Good Friday trial'.

In 1538 Becket's shrine was destroyed on the orders of Henry VIII and the remains of the saint were burnt.

But he has never been forgotten and in 2003 Pope John Paul II, when receiving Archbishop Rowan Williams, 'vividly' recalled 'the moving experience of praying at the tomb of St Thomas Becket'.

On St Thomas Becket's Day 2003 Irish-born Papal Nuncio Archbishop Michael Courtney was assassinated in Burundi. 'In the footsteps of Christ, the Good Shepherd, he sacrificed himself for the people of Burundi, where the Pope had sent him as an apostle of peace,' said Cardinal Angelo Sodano.

Relics

Canterbury's Roman Catholic Church also has a small bone which was taken from the body in 1220 and survived in Italy. There is also a tiny piece of black clothing - possibly his Benedictine habit. Alongside are some vestments which belonged to Archbishop Oscar Romero of San Salvador who in 1980 was also assassinated in church by shady government agents. A relic of Thomas, given to the church by a descendant of one of the knights, was presented to San Salvador Cathedral.

London's Westminster Cathedral has St Thomas's mitre and shoulder blade relics. St George's Cathedral in Southwark possesses a tiny relic.

A fragment of Becket's skull is kept at Stonyhurst College where it is venerated today and another at Angers Cathedral in France.

Part of an elbow is in Hungary's Esztergom Cathedral having been taken from the body at Canterbury in 1220 when it was moved upstairs.

Anagni Cathedral in Italy was visited by St Thomas and one of his mitres survives in the museum.

The Ladyewell Shrine near Preston in Lancashire has recently received relics brought back from Italy.

In Church

Pope John XXIII raised today to the rank of a First Class Feast observed throughout the world. However, in 2001 the day officially became an Optional Memorial. Since 2010 it has been a feast in the English and Wales calendar. According to the Anglican Church's Common Worship today is Lesser Festival. Vestments are red. The opening prayer is:

> *Lord God,*
> *who gave grace to your servant Thomas Becket*
> *to put aside all earthly fear and be faithful even to death;*
> *grant that we,*
> *disregarding worldly esteem,*
> *may fight all wrong, uphold your rule,*
> *and serve you to our life's end.*
> *We ask this through our Lord Jesus Christ, your Son,*
> *who lives and reigns with you in the unity of the Holy Spirit,*
> *God for ever and ever.*
> *Amen*

It is appropriate to pray for those in high office in church and state.

Today at Canterbury

At the Cathedral the venue for the early Eucharist is the Altar of the Swordpoint on the martyrdom site. The celebrant is usually the Archbishop vested in a replica Becket red chasuble.

Solemn evensong at 3.15pm enacts liturgically the events of 29 December 1170. The service, usually with the Archbishop presiding, begins in the Quire. After the first lesson, the clergy and congregation, holding lighted candles, move to the Martyrdom. Here there is the first of three readings from T. S. Eliot's *Murder in the Cathedral* play which had its première in the chapter house in 1935. The Altar of the Swordpoint is censed during the singing of the Magnificat. Following the second lesson there is another excerpt from the play during which the doors from the cloister are banged shut and then, at Becket's cry 'throw open the doors!', banged open. Since Becket's body was taken to the crypt after Vespers so today's procession continues to the Undercroft for the Nunc Dimittis, a final reading and prayers.

Later in the evening Canterbury's Roman Catholic congregation sings Vespers in the Undercroft. Mass at the Roman Catholic Church of St Thomas of Canterbury is at noon.

Other Events

At Mottola, in Italy's Puglia, Becket is the patron saint with a chapel in the cathedral where he is depicted in a 14th-century fresco. This evening the keys of the city are handed over to the patron saint in an outdoor ceremony followed by Mass in the Cathedral. On the eve of the festival there is an extravagant musical pageant loosely based on T. S. Eliot's play *Murder in the Cathedral* involving three hundred costumed participants in procession with drums, flaming torches and flags.

Layana in Spain's Aragon region has St Thomas as the town's patron and celebrates today by making sweet flat bread known as Farinosos.

Esztergom Cathedral near Budapest in Hungary displays relics brought by Becket's friend Cardinal Lukacs Banffy.

The Translation of St James

30 December

Today another who become a companion of Jesus in his ministry is remembered. This feast, first found in Spain's Mozarabic Rite calendar, marks the moving of St James the Great's body from the Holy Land to Spain. It was the St James the Great feast day until 1080 when the Mozarabic liturgy gave way to the Roman. Then the celebration of his martyrdom moved to 25 July in the warmer part of the year and the December date became the day to commemorate both the calling of James by Jesus at the Sea of Galilee and the arrival, many years after death, of his beheaded body at Padron, a small river port near Santiago.

St James

St James the Great was brother of St John (see page 94) and like him also an Apostle. Both were Galilean fishermen and among the first to be called by Christ. Both could be described as being in the inner circle. James witnessed the Transfiguration of Christ on Mount Tabor and was close to Jesus in the garden of Gethsemane on the first Maundy Thursday. Eleven years later James was the first Apostle to be martyred when Agrippa I had him beheaded (Acts 12.2). He is the only Apostle to have his death recorded in the Gospels. Around 814 the body is said to have been taken from Jerusalem to the port of Jaffa and placed in a ship carrying stone as ballast to Spain. The saint's bones are now in Santiago de Compostela Cathedral in Galicia, north-west Spain.

The authenticity of the remains has been subject to debate. However, the bones in Santiago do lack a right hand which is in keeping with the biblical record of James's death when his raised hand was cut off before the beheading. A hand, thought to be that of St James, was once kept in Reading Abbey and this is possibly the hand now in the possession of St Peter's Church in Marlow, Buckinghamshire. The head of St James is buried in the Armenian Cathedral of St James on the execution site in Jerusalem.

Pilgrimage

Santiago is the third most important place of Christian pilgrimage after the Holy Land and Rome and the focal point of long and ancient pilgrim routes walked by thousands every year.

The tomb of St James was discovered in Spain's Galicia early in the 9th century and Santiago Cathedral was built over the site. Pilgrimage to Santiago was popular by the 12th century and a series of monasteries and refuges was built along the pilgrim roads. The four main routes, merging to pass through Burgos and Léon to Santiago, were described in the first known guide book, *Liber Sancti Jacobi*, written during 12th century.

An English route runs from the port of La Corûna on the northern Spanish coast and can be covered on foot in three days. Ships linked to such ports as Poole in Dorset.

Today there is the same chain of hospitality with foot pilgrims having their camino passport stamped along the main routes in order to be able to exchange it for a 'compostela' (certificate) at Santiago. St James Garlickhythe Church in London has a stamp available for those starting out from the capital. The pilgrim emblem is a scallop shell which appears on buildings and waymarks along the routes.

Pilgrims can obtain a 'passport' from the Confraternity of St James, Christ Church, 27 Blackfriars Road, London SE1 8NY. www.csj.org.uk

In The Bible

St Mark 1.16-20 and St Luke 5.10
James was called by Christ along with fellow fishermen Andrew,

Peter and James's own brother John. He was present at the Transfiguration and with Christ in the Garden of at Gethsemane (St Matthew 17.1-27, 26. 37 and St Mark 5.37). He died by beheading (Acts 12.2).

In Church

This is an optional feast with readings as for St James's Day (25 July). The vestments are red.

Today at St James's Tomb

The morning Mass at Santiago Cathedral is at noon but is preceded at 11.40am by a procession round the cathedral with a figure of St James holding a tiny relic. Immediately afterwards the *botafumeiro* – a huge censer – is swung from the roof of the crossing. Following the creed, the Royal representative (who might be the mayor or speaker of the regional parliament) makes the offering to St James in the form of a speech touching on contemporary matters and invoking the help of the saint for the nation –St James is Spain's patron saint. The Archbishop's response, or homily, follows. In 1109 Alphonso VI was at the cathedral on 30 December to make the first offering of two dozen gold and silver coins. Philip IV reintroduced the ceremony custom in 1646. King Juan Carlos and Queen Sofia attended in person in 2003 when the day marked the start of a Santiago Holy Year. St James's Day (25 July) next falls on a Sunday, making a Holy Year, in 2021.

Mozarabic celebrations

St James's Day Mass is celebrated in the Mozarabic rite today at Toledo Cathedral and at the church of Santiago el Mayor in Seville.

Holy Family is transferred to today when 1 January falls on a Sunday.

The Holy Family Sunday
Sunday after Christmas Day

Holy Family was instituted by Pope Leo XIII in 1893 and observed on the Sunday after The Epiphany until moved by Pope John XXIII to the Sunday following Christmas Day.

The most famous church dedicated to the Holy Family is the Sagrada Familia in Barcelona. The idea of the church came from bookseller Josep María Bocabella who was inspired by the church at Loreto. However the final extraordinary design, bearing no relation, is by the Catalan architect Antoni Gaudi who died in 1926. Although not complete, the basilica was consecrated by Pope Benedict XVI in 2010.

Many Anglican Churches keep Holy Family Sunday but for those observing the First Sunday of Christmas there is reference to family in the post communion prayer: '... help your church to live as one family, united in love and obedience'.

Holy Family is transferred to 30 December to make way for Solemnity of Mary Mother of God when 1 January falls on a Sunday as in 2023.

New Year's Eve
St Sylvester's Day
31 December

New Year's Eve is known just as St Sylvester's Day in many European countries including Belgium, Germany, France (la Fete de Saint-Sylvestre), Italy, Poland and Switzerland.

St Sylvester

Sylvester, one of the first non-martyrs to be given a feast day, was elected Pope in 314 and died today in 335. His reign coincided with the Church's first period free from persecution following the difficult years of the Roman Emperor Diocletian when St Nicholas (see page 27), St Lucy (see page 48) and St Agnes (see page 148) died. Emperor Constantine gave the Lateran Palace to be Rome's cathedral which Sylvester consecrated in about 324. He also built the first St Peter's Basilica and the first St Agnes in Agone Church in the Piazza Navona. Indeed it may be that Sylvester encouraged the Emperor to erect several magnificent Christian buildings in Rome making it visibly the centre of the Christian world.

Sylvester's remains, moved from a basilica above the Catacomb of Priscilla to the new San Silvestro in Capite in 761, are beneath a Michelangelo-designed high altar. The church's name means St Sylvester at the Head which is a reference to John the Baptist's head in a chapel by the entrance.

In 1895 the church was assigned by Pope Leo XIII to the English and is served by Irish Pallottine Fathers. It was the titular church of Archbishop Basil Hume of Westminster when he became a cardinal and he was succeeded by Cardinal

Desmond Connell of Dublin.

Prince Charles Edward Stuart, Bonnie Prince Charlie, was born on 31 December 1720 and given the name Sylvester. The saint is portrayed by Evelyn Waugh in his historical novel *Helena*.

In Church
St Sylvester's Day is an optional commemoration.

Watchnight Service
Some churches have a watchnight service at about 11.30pm to enable people to see in the new year in church. In the West Indies it is the custom to have a midnight Mass.

Watchnight services became popular during the last half of the 19th century. The first may have been at St Alban's Holborn in about 1863 when a crowd gathered outside the new church causing the clergy to get out of bed. Young curate Arthur Stanton unlocked the church and made the service an annual event. On 31 December 1911 Fr Arthur Stanton, still curate and near the end of his life, described the church as always 'choke-full' on that night but added: 'They have a superstition that it is lucky to see the New Year in, in church. That is all.'

In 1905 a huge noisy crowd, including many soldiers, is recorded as having gathered outside nearby St Paul's Cathedral singing 'Auld Lang Syne' and the National Anthem just before midnight when the chimes of Great Tom were met with cheers. This became an annual custom until 1936 when the cathedral finally opened its doors for a watchnight service. The tradition continued until 2007.

The popularity of the watchnight service spread across the world when the BBC Overseas Service broadcast one regularly from the St Martin-in-the-Fields.

Today at St Sylvester's Tomb
In 1910 the *Tablet* described San Silvestro in Capite as 'a sacred magnet…on the last day of the year'. Today Mass is in Italian at 6pm followed by a sung Te Deum.

Other Celebrations

In Rome the Pope presides at first vespers of the Solemnity of Mary, Mother of God and a Te Deum of thanksgiving for the end of the year in St Peter's.

Wesley's Chapel in London's City Road has a watch night service from 11pm. Midnight Mass at St George's Cathedral in Southwark, a tradition started in 2000, begins at 11pm and ends shortly before the fireworks display on the nearby South Bank.

In Stockholm on every New Year's Eve since 1895 Tennyson's poem 'Ring Out Wild Bells', which reflects on the dying year, has been recited in Swedish just before midnight at Skansen outdoor museum by a well-known Swede. The words are part of *In Memoriam* and the bells are those of Waltham Abbey built as a penance for the murder of Thomas Becket (see page 96). The Skansen celebrations and fireworks, which attract thousands of visitors, are televised live.

In Vienna crowds gather in the square outside the cathedral to hear the Pummerin bell rung at the stroke of midnight. It was cast from Turkish cannon and, apart from New Year's Eve, is only rung on special occasions such as St Stephen's Day (see page 88) or the death of the Archbishop.

New Year's Day

Solemnity of Mary, Mother of God
World Day of Prayer for Peace
Naming and Circumcision of Jesus
1 January

This, the first day of the new year and World Day of Prayer for Peace, is dedicated to Jesus' Mother, Mary.

In the 7th century today, the end of the octave or eight days of Christmas but not a New Year, was known as the Commemoration of Holy Mary. By the 14th century it had become the Circumcision of the Lord which made sense as Jewish tradition was for a boy to be circumcised on the eighth day. However, in 1969 Pope Paul VI reverted to the original celebration by declaring New Year's Day to be the Solemnity of Mary, the Holy Mother of God, the commemoration of the conferral of the Most Holy Name of Jesus and World Day of Prayer for Peace. In 2002 the Holy Name was transferred as an option to 3 January. For Anglicans today remains the Naming and Circumcision of Jesus. Lutherans keep it as just the Holy Name of Jesus.

Today has been a holiday throughout the United Kingdom only since 1975 although Scotland has enjoyed it since 1871.

Solemnity of Mary, Mother of God

In 1969 the Motherhood of Mary, which for many years had been observed on 11 October, was moved to New Year's Day when it could be kept in the context of Christmas. It is also nearer to the feast's original date and reinstates an old tradition of the year beginning on a day associated with Mary. The Annunciation 25 March was once New Year's Day.

World Day of Prayer for Peace

On 1 January 1968 Pope Paul VI said that it was his desire that the year should start with a peace day 'as a sign of hope and promise, at the beginning of the calendar which measures and guides the journey of human life through time, in order that peace, with its just and salutary equilibrium, will dominate the unfolding of history yet to come'. The first World Day of Prayer for Peace on 1 January 1969 had the theme 'To Reach Peace, Teach Peace'. The 1993 theme was 'If You Want Peace, Reach Out to the Poor' and in 2002 'No Peace Without Justice, No Justice Without Peace'. For 2007 Pope Benedict chose 'The Human Family, a Community of Peace'. The Pope celebrates Mass this morning in St Peter's Basilica and preaches on the year's peace theme. Diplomats accredited to the Holy See are invited to attend.

In The Bible

St Luke 2.21

St Luke records Jesus being circumcised on the eighth day although no details or location are given. However, circumcision was normal on the eighth day after birth. Luke also emphasises that Jesus received the name communicated by the Angel to Mary when she became pregnant (see page 42).

In Church

The Gospel reading (Luke 2: 16-21) provides a link to the old observance by including the reference to the circumcision.

The Most Holy Name of Jesus

3 January

Today's optional designation celebrates the Christ Child being named Jesus as directed by God through the angel at the Annunciation. Jesus in Hebrew means 'The Lord saves'.

The special day, long kept on different dates including 1 and 2 January (see page 113), has been an option for today in the Roman Catholic Church since 2002.

The Jesuit church serving the university community in Manchester and the Roman Catholic church at Oundle in Northamptonshire are dedicated to The Most Holy Name of Jesus.

THE EPIPHANY

Eve of Epiphany
The Twelfth Night
5 January

Tomorrow is the Epiphany when the arrival of the Three Kings at Bethlehem is recalled (see page 122). Tonight used to be called Twelfth Night. However by the time of the Restoration in the mid-17th century it had become the custom to keep Twelfth Night on 6 January when the Christmas decorations are taken down. Samuel Pepys wrote on 6 January 1665: 'At night home, being Twelfthnight, and there chose my piece of cake.' But tonight is certainly Twelfth Night abroad.

Twelfth Night Cakes

Enjoyed tonight in Spanish homes is a ring shaped twisted sweet bread called Rosca de Reyes symbolising a crown with cherries and other fruits on top being the jewels. Inside is a baby figurine. In Mexico whoever is served the slice with the baby by tradition hosts the party at Candlemas (see page 155). It has been suggested that the Christ Child is hidden in the bread to symbolise the hiding of the infant from King Herod's soldiers (see page 95). The cake in Spain sometimes comes with cream and also a paper crown for the person who finds the baby.

In New Orleans a plastic baby is included in the round sweet breads called King Cakes and decorated with the yellow, green and purple colours of Mardi Gras to provide a link to Lent which leads to Good Friday and Easter.

In Provence the twelfth night cake is puff pastry in the shape of a crown decorated with crystallised fruits. In much of France many people buy a flat almond cream pastry cake called a Galette de Rois with a trinket known as a fève since the original trinket was a *fève* or fava bean. The person who finds the trinket in their slice becomes king or queen for the evening and wears a paper crown. The recipe dates from the Middle Ages but in the late 19th century small porcelain figurines began to replace beans. Now fèves include the figures of Mickey Mouse and Harry Potter.

This tradition may go back to the Roman Saturnalia when a slave could find a token or bean in a cake and be crowned King of Misrule. In the 11th century the monks of Besançon Abbey, now the university, chose their abbot by putting coin in a loaf.

In Germany an iced Three Kings cake, a Dreikönigskuchen with a small foil crown, is eaten tonight.

English cakes were usually an iced fruit cake with a pea or another small item hidden inside for choosing the king or queen of the party. In 1669 Samuel Pepys staged a draw 'to prevent spoiling the cake' and by accident drew out a card making him queen for the night. During the early 19th century large Twelfth Night cakes, often known as just Twelfth Cakes, were still proudly displayed in bakers' windows. On 6 January 1848 architect Augustus Pugin celebrated in the evening with a cake and the selection of a king and queen. Charles Dickens enjoyed the cake as did Queen Victoria but by the end of her reign the Twelfth Night cake had been superseded by the Christmas cake eaten on Christmas Day.

However, a Twelfth Night cake is shared annually by the cast at London's Theatre Royal, Drury Lane after the curtain falls tomorrow night. The will of actor Robert Baddeley, who died in 1794, provided for the cake now known as the Baddeley Cake. On Twelfth Night 1763 he had found fellow players looking glum because they were not at a party so he sent out for a Twelfth Night cake from The Strand. The tradition is also maintained at the The Old Vic on the nearest Saturday afternoon when an actor from the current production presides at the cutting ceremony started by Lilian Baylis in 1923.

Today's Events

Spain

In Spain today, eve of the Day of the Kings (El Día de Los Reyes), there are processions in the early evening involving three individuals dressed as the Three Kings and sometimes arriving on camels. This tradition began in Alcoy in 1866 and has taken place annually since 1885. Here the Kings arrive on camels and present their gifts to the Nativity scene accompanied by Handel's music. Seville's procession dates from just 1916. At Canada in Alicante the Three Kings make their way through fields to the town. At Barcelona the Three Kings arrive by boat and parade through the streets throwing sweets to children. Helpers in Madrid's procession distribute 7,000 tons of sweets to huge crowds lining the streets. The Kings who ride on individual floats were until 2015 members of the city council selected by lot from the different political parties. The Kings are now played by actors including a black male in the role of the traditional black King. In 2016 two suburbs controversially introduced a Queen as one of the three as part of the move towards diversity.

Children write letters to the Kings and find gifts supposedly left by them early on Epiphany morning. Tomorrow is still the main day for exchanging presents which means that Spanish shops remain decorated during the twelve days of Christmas rather than switching to January sales on 26 December.

Italy

In Italy today is called Epifania or Befana. Children put out a stocking tonight to find it in the morning filled with presents by the mythical figure of La Befana - an old lady with a witch-style broom who is said to have been sweeping her house when the Three Kings asked the way to the Baby Jesus. Once naughty children risked receiving a piece of coal but today all children get a sugar coal. Decorations often include the broom.

The Epiphany

6 January

The Epiphany, the climax of the twelve days of Christmas, celebrates the first manifestation of Christ when the Three Kings, or Wise Men, are said to have arrived in Bethlehem led by the star and bringing presents of gold, frankincense and myrrh. The three, by tradition from different lands, were the first non-Jews to see and acknowledge Christ.

The shepherds calling at the stable on Christmas morning represent the people of Israel. The kings represent all other ethnic and language groups who are also the people of God.

The other manifestations are the Baptism of Christ thirty years later, marked next Sunday, and the first miracle when Jesus, at the instigation of his mother Mary, turned water into wine at the wedding in Cana near his home town of Nazareth (John 2.1-11). St John's account of Cana is today's evening prayer New Testament reading and will often be the gospel reading on one of the Sundays between the Baptism and Candlemas.

The Epiphany, older than Christmas Day, was also the feast of the incarnation until around 337 when Christmas Day was included in the Roman calendar.

King Harold was crowned on 6 January in 1066 and later Henry VIII chose the day to marry his third wife Anne of Cleves. Ben Jonson wrote four Twelfth Night masques for James I whose son Henry was made Prince of Wales on the Epiphany 1610.

It was a time of great feasting for everyone. During the Tudor period, the lay community of St Bartholomew Hospital in Sandwich had a candlelit Twelfth Night dinner which involved purchasing beef, prunes, raisins, saffron, cloves, mace and beer.

Meanwhile the Morris men dancing outside the church enjoyed refreshments such as 'some new cheese, some old cheese,' flans, tarts and ale.

Today is a public holiday in Austria, Finland, Greece, Italy, Spain, Sweden and, again since 2011 after a fifty year gap, in Poland. The Irish still sometimes call today Women's Christmas as the men by tradition once took over domestic duties. But in Britain the Epiphany is now largely ignored. Indeed, not only do Christmas cards tend to show the shepherds and Three Kings all crowded into the stable together, but since 2007 the Roman Catholic Church in England and Wales has kept the Epiphany on the nearest Sunday which can be as early as 2 January or as late as 8 January.

Tonight, as the western church celebrates the Epiphany, the Russian Orthodox Church and the Coptic Church are keeping Christmas Eve.

What Happened Today
Matthew 2.1-12
Three Wise Men or kings, also known as the Magi, were led by a star, to pay homage to Jesus at Bethlehem. They brought gold, frankincense and myrrh as presents.

The Star
The role of the star is a mystery although the conjunction of Saturn and Jupiter in November 7BC would have been visible over Bethlehem. Some look to an attempt to fulfil the words in Numbers 24.17 where there is reference to a star emerging from Jacob. The word 'Magi', sometimes used for the Kings, means Persian astrologers. If the Magi was led by a star they may have been following it months before Christ was born.

They are recorded as saying they had seen the star in the east before arriving in Jerusalem (Matthew 2.2). A comet could exist and be observed eighteen months before the birth and therefore before Mary was aware of her condition. If they were astronomers rather than astrologers they may have been following a star others would not normally have seen. According to Matthew (2.5) the star led first to Jerusalem where the chief priests pointed the way to nearby Bethlehem by quoting the prophetic announcement found in Micah (5:1): 'Bethlehem… from you will come a leader.'

Astronomer Patrick Moore was convinced that the Magi had observed two meteors following the same path which would not have been widely seen by others less interested in astronomy.

It may be that following the star meant following astrological deductions which led to Bethlehem. Speaking in 2012, Fr Guy Consolmagno SJ of the Vatican Observatory said: 'We do not know what the star of Bethlehem was. We were not there. Whether it was a planetary conjunction, a miracle or a pious parable, ultimately the explanation does not matter. The real star of Matthew's account is the person it leads us to.'

Three Kings

The Bible mentions the Kings but does not say how many there were. Some translations suggest Wise Men. The earliest representation is 3rd-century in Rome's Catacomb of Priscilla and depicts three multi-cultural figures. In the 6th century they were depicted in mosaic in Ravenna's Basilica of Sant' Apollinare Nuovo representing young, middle aged and old. At the same time they received, from an Armenian gospel, the names of Melchior, Balthasar and Caspar. Later, in an attempt to represent all nations, it became the custom to depict one as black.

The idea, not mentioned in the New Testament, that they arrived on camels owes much to a passage in the Old Testament (Isaiah 60.6) understood as foretelling the event.

Matthew writes of them coming from the 'east' which probably means outside the Roman Empire and most likely Persia. They could have made a 2,000 mile round journey across Iran (Persia), Iraq and Jordan. The city of Saveh, where there is evidence of early Christian worship, is claimed by some Iranians to be both their starting point and their burial place.

They are sometimes called Magi which would indicate that

they may have been elite Persians specialising in interpreting dreams and signs of the future.

Tarshish, the area around Huelva in Spain's Andalusia region, is sometimes said to be a starting point due to a mention in Psalm 72 along with Sheba (Yemen) and Seba (a city on the River Nile). Sheba is also listed in Isaiah along with Midian (Saudi Arabia) and Ephah (Qatar and other nearby countries). Tur Abdin in today's eastern Turkey claims that the Three Kings rested there on their return journey under the assumption that the three came from the same place.

St Helena, mother of the Emperor Constantine, discovered their alleged bones and took them to Constantinople. Shortly afterwards the relics were moved to St Eustorgio's Church in Milan where there is still an empty tomb. After the Holy Roman Emperor had captured the city he gave the remains to Cologne and so in 1164 its Archbishop took them over the Alps to a huge welcome in the German city. Today the relics are in a large reliquary in Cologne Cathedral which is topped not with a cross but a star.

Cloth with the bones has been dated to the first century and in 2005 Pope Benedict was able to say at the cathedral: 'Here in Cologne one of the Magi has been identified as a Moorish King of Africa, so that a representative of the African continent has been seen as one of Christ's first witnesses.'

Gold

This was even more valuable than it is today and the gift indicates that Jesus is Christ the King. The gold, if in the form of Roman gold colour coins, may have paid the bill for the inn or the Holy Family's safe passage to Egypt.

Frankincense

This recognises Christ as God since it was a symbol of a divine name. Frankincense is high quality incense which was widely available in Sheba (see above). The burning of incense in the stable may have improved the air for the Holy Family. The gum resin, derived from beneath the bark of trees growing in semi-desert, was considered precious. Christ would later know incense through the Psalms with such references as 'Let my prayer be counted as incense before you, and the lifting up of my hands as an evening sacrifice' (114. 2). He would also come to see incense being burned in the Temple and because the Magi brought incense to Christ so incense has long been burnt in church when Christ is present in the Eucharist. Incense represents prayers rising to God but it is the smell rather than the smoke which is important and adding it to worship is an act of love for Christ in the manner of the woman who broke ointment over Christ on the eve of Palm Sunday. In 1866 the newly opened St Alban's Holborn chose today as the most appropriate time to introduce the regular use of incense.

Myrrh

This represents the death of Jesus to come 33 years later. On Good Friday myrrh mixed with wine was offered to Jesus on the cross and afterwards Nicodemus, who helped to move Christ's dead body from the cross to the tomb, arrived with myrrh to embalm the body. Mary who today holds Baby Jesus in her arms will again hold his body after his death.

Relics

St Paul's monastery on Mount Athos holds the alleged gifts of the Kings in the form of gold in frames and a mixture of frankincense and myrrh. They are said to have been retained by the Virgin Mary and remained in Jerusalem until about 400 after which they were in Constantinople. The monastery received them in the 15th century. In this present century the items have been displayed in Athens and briefly taken to Russia.

In Church

Incense is often used at this Mass and to cense the crib which should now have kings rather than shepherds in the scene.

The traditional gifts of gold, frankincense and myrrh, or representations, may be placed at the crib.

The first reading from Isaiah (60.1-6) mentions camels travelling in the desert and gifts of gold and frankincense. A suitable hymn is *Songs of thankfulness and praise* which embraces the Magi as 'sages from afar', baptism's 'Jordan's stream' and the first miracle 'water into wine'. *I saw three ships* refers to the arrival of the Magi's relics at Cologne on the River Rhine.

The hymn *We three kings of Orient are* has a verse dedicated to myrrh and death. This is often sung whilst gold, frankincense and myrrh are carried in procession to the crib. Author Mary Kenny has pointed out that the tune 'is written to chime perfectly with the cadence of a camel's pace'.

The crucifixion of Christ is also alluded to in *Bethlehem, of noblest cities*, written about 400 by Roman Spaniard Aurelius Prudentius, with the verse: 'Solemn things of mystic meaning:/ Incense doth the God disclose,/ Gold a royal child proclaimeth,/ Myrrh a future tomb foreshows.'

St Peter's in Rome often has young teenagers, male and female, in the congregation dressed as kings and taking part in the offertory procession both today and on 1 January.

Sometimes chalk is blessed for members of the congregation to take home and use to write C+M+B over their front door indicating that if the Three Kings were to call at the house they would find Jesus in the hearts of the occupants. The capital letters are the initials of the Three Kings but can also mean 'Christus mansionem benedictat' (Christ bless this house).

The main Christmas decorations often come down late tonight in church as well as home although the crib, with just the Holy Family in place, can remain until Candlemas. Some churches keep the Christmas tree in place, although maybe not decorated, until next Sunday or even Candlemas.

In some cathedrals and larger churches it is the tradition to announce today the dates of Lent and Easter. This custom dates from at least the 4th century when astronomers in Alexandria, having determined the date, communicated the year's calendar to the Patriarchs and later Rome. The proclamation helps link Christmas to Holy Week and the Resurrection by including the words: 'Let us recall the year's culmination, the Easter Triduum of the Lord: his last supper, his crucifixion, his burial, and his rising ...'

Today in Bethlehem

There is a solemn Mass in the Church of the Nativity at 10am. Vespers at 3.30pm is followed by a procession, representing the arrival of the Magi, down into the Grotto of the Nativity.

Today at the Three Kings' Tomb

There are two main masses celebrated before the Shrine of the Three Kings in Cologne Cathedral where three large candles, each decorated with a crown and marked C, B and M, burn. At the end of the always very well-attended 10am Pontifical Solemn Mass, groups of children dressed as the kings and holding a star on the end of a pole gather before the central altar to sing carols. Afterwards they process with the Archbishop out into the square to sing and collect money for charity. During day the sanctuary is open to the public to view the Three Kings Shrine and light candles in stands at the chancel steps. At 6.30pm there is another Pontifical Solemn Mass followed by a procession involving the entire congregation round the cathedral to the shrine at the east end where a halt is made for the Archbishop to cense the golden reliquary box.

Other Epiphany Events

At the St James's Palace chapel in London an offering of gold, frankincense and myrrh is made on behalf of the Queen during an 11am Sung Eucharist. This was once a major occasion with the monarch present, wearing the Crown, and accompanied by the Knights of the Garter, Thistle and Bath. The last King to present the gifts in person was George II in 1757. The following year Princess Caroline was buried on the eve of the Epiphany and George asked the Lord Chamberlain to deputise for him.

Now the Queen is always at Sandringham in January.

During the offertory the Queen's representatives carry the gifts on two 1821 silver salvers from Brighton's Chapel Royal and hands them to the Sub Dean who in turn hands them to the Bishop of London. The aisle is lined by the Yeomen of the Guard who have replaced the Heralds present when the monarch attended. The gold is 25 new coins borrowed from the Bank of England. Until 1859 a silk bag contained a small roll leaf of gold but the new sovereigns (on a dish) were introduced at the Prince Consort's suggestion. The frankincense and myrrh (on one dish) are supplied by the Queen's Apothecary and afterwards the frankincense is sent to a church whilst the latter goes to Elmore Abbey, the Anglican Benedictine community, to be mixed with the incense made there. Admission is by ticket obtained by writing in October to the Chapel Royal, St James's Palace, London SW1A 1BS.

In Manchester on the nearest Sunday evening, clergy and choristers set out from the city's St Ann's Church in procession led by a star to the cathedral. Three people are dressed as kings whilst others carry lanterns.

A very old Epiphany custom takes place at Haxey, on the Isle of Axholme in Lincolnshire, where villagers from three pubs and the Carpenters Arms in nearby Westwoodside compete to carry a hood (2ft long, 3 inch diameter, leather cylinder) back to one of the pubs. The origin is maybe an incident in the 14th century when a gust of wind blew a hood off Lady de Mowbray who was riding on the Epiphany. However, the earliest account of the game is only found in 1815.

At 2.30pm the Lord of the Hood, 13 Boggins (who act as referees and represent those who chased the original hood) arrive with the Fool in procession at St Nicholas Church, the 'cathedral of the Isle'. The Fool (the successor of the person who caught the hood) makes a speech from a mounting block until smoke from burning wet straw at the base overwhelms him. All chant 'Hoose agen hoose, toon agen toon, if tha meets a man nok im doon, but doant ot im' ('House against House, Town against Town, if you meets a man, knock him down but don't hurt him') before he leads everyone to Hood Field. At about 3.30pm, after hood games for young people, the main hood is thrown to the crowd. The struggle can take two to eight hours and involve about 50 people with several hundred spectators who can be called upon by either village side. The mainly male melée, the Sway, abides by a rule that the hood cannot be kicked or thrown. As normal laws are ignored cars can be overturned and even walls demolished under the weight of the crowd but any damage is strictly put right afterwards.

Each year the Lord of the Hood has a new willow wand of office -made of 13 branches to represent the boggins and one short one for the fool, bound thirteen times together. The word 'boggin' may be derived from the 'bog' which surrounded the isle. Afterwards the winning pub pours beer over the Hood and hangs it behind the bar for the year. The game takes place on Saturday 5 January when the Epiphany falls on a Sunday.

In the Italian city of Florence a 15th-century custom of staging a lavish Cavalcade of the Magi, abandoned when the Medici family was expelled from Florence in 1494, was restored in 1997. Il Cavalcata dei Magi, a long costumed procession involving 700 people but without the Magi, sets out at 2.15pm from the Pitti Palace to cross the Ponte Vecchio where it is joined by standard bearers. The main participants are dressed in costumes based on Benozzo Gozzoli's 1459 fresco *The Procession of the Magi* in the chapel at the Palazzo Medici-Riccardi. On arrival at the cathedral there is an outdoor reading from St Matthew's Gospel and an address by the Archbishop. Afterwards, as dusk approaches, the kings arrive on horseback to present their gifts at the real life manger complete with sheep which reflects not only the painting but the live crib introduced by St Frances of Assisi in 1223.

In the Polish capital Warsaw there is a Three Kings procession to a live crib scene, first held in 2009, which starts with the Angelus at noon in Castle Square. Similar events take place elsewhere in Poland.

The Baptism of The Lord

The Sunday after The Epiphany

This Sunday, the final part of the Epiphany celebration, looks beyond the early days to Christ's baptism by John the Baptist, which took place when Jesus was aged 30. It marked the start of his earthly ministry. This special Sunday was introduced in 1969 so that the Baptism could be observed within the octave of the Epiphany rather than be forgotten on the Epiphany itself when the Wise Men take centre stage.

In some places today is also Plough Sunday.

Baptism Site

In Israel there has been a Baptism site by the River Jordan for many years which pilgrims have visited although it was not known to be the actual spot. However in 1996 archaeologists working downstream in the Kingdom of Jordan discovered hillside marble steps leading down to a dry river bed which sometimes flooded. This site, known as Bethany beyond the Jordan, is now where John the Baptist is thought most likely to have lived, preached and probably baptised Christ. It is where St John's Gospel (1.28) locates the event. During land mine clearing, the remains of two churches, three caves and three baptism pools were discovered. The site was visited by Popes John Paul II, Benedict and Francis.

Plough Sunday

Ancient Plough Monday tomorrow was the inspiration in 1943 for Plough Sunday which was introduced on the Sunday after The Epiphany to encourage wartime food production. At this time today was the Sunday after Epiphany rather than Baptism

Sunday. There are a number of village churches where ploughs or symbolic ancient ploughs are still blessed during the main service and prayers said for a good harvest and for those who work on the land.

In The Bible

Matthew 3.13-17, Mark 1.7-11, Luke 3.15-22 and John 1.19-28.

Jesus travelled from his home town of Nazareth to be baptised in the River Jordan by his cousin John the Baptist. John was surprised and reluctant to baptise someone he recognised to be Christ. Followers of John's preaching were also baptised but, after Jesus had been in the river or pool, the Holy Spirit as a dove descended on Christ.

In Church

Mass may begin with a sprinkling of holy water as a reminder of baptism. Tonight many cathedrals and churches hold Epiphany Carol services involving processions and sometimes figures dressed as the Three Kings. This is often the last day for the Christmas Tree and decorations to be displayed. If the tree remains it may already have been stripped of its decorations and lights.

Baptism Events

In the Greek Orthodox Church, which unlike Russia keeps the Western dates for Christmas, there is a greater emphasis on the Baptism of Christ at Epiphany. St John Chrysostom spoke of water receiving sanctification because of Christ's baptism and this is highlighted by the tradition of the blessing of baptismal water and the throwing of a cross into a river or the sea at Epiphany or today. The young boy chosen to dive into the icy water and retrieve it is said to enjoy good luck for the year.

Members of the Greek Orthodox Church at Westgate-on-Sea in Kent gather on nearby Margate beach this morning for the blessing of the waters ceremony. The custom began here in 1964 and in 2010 Archbishop of Canterbury Rowan Williams joined the Archbishop Gregorios of Thyateira and Great Britain for the annual occasion. This takes place on the Epiphany when 6 January falls on a Sunday.

After the main morning services, the congregations of St Magnus on the north end of London Bridge and Southwark Cathedral on the south bank meet at the parish boundary on the bridge for the Blessing of the Waters. A wooden cross is thrown into the river. This custom began in 2004.

In a tradition started in 1983 by Blessed John Paul, the Pope baptises a number of babies during a Solemn Mass in the Sistine Chapel. John Paul christened as many as twenty from several nations on this Sunday whilst Pope Francis has allowed the number to rise to more than thirty.

Plough Sunday Events

Plough Sunday observance at St Andrew's Kirkby Malzeard, near Ripon, was first held in 1947 and involves farmers carrying a plough into church. The service ends with a sword dance.

A Blessing of the Plough service is held at St Mary's in Goathland, Yorkshire, after a replica plough has been dragged through the streets. Next Saturday is Day of the Dance for Goathland Plough Stots who in a 200 year old tradition perform a sword dance around the village.

This morning's Plough Sunday service at Newark parish church is preceded by a civic procession from the Town Hall and the placing of a plough and milk churn in church.

Thaxted Church in Essex, in addition to the 10am Sunday Eucharist, has a Plough Sunday Service attended by the Thaxted Morris and followed by a ploughman's lunch.

Since 2008 St Edmundsbury Cathedral has marked Plough Sunday with the blessing of a plough and tractor following evensong.

St Giles Ludlow revived the observance in 2016.

Plough Monday
Monday after 6 January

Plough Monday recalls the time when this was the first day back to work after the Christmas holiday.

The custom of dressing up on Plough Monday in ribbons or a garment of straw and collecting money, at first for church candles, dates back to 1378 but was mainly confined to the East Midlands, the Fens and Yorkshire. The figure would dance in the streets, collect money and be well supplied with beer as he was led on a rope from pub to pub. At the end of the 19th century farmworkers still performed a door to door play around Collingham in Nottinghamshire.

The tradition of a final day off today was once widespread. In Belgium, especially around Tournai, today is known has been known as Lost Monday since the 13th century because people lost income taking the day off. Now residents come together in parties to share a rabbit and prune casserole and, with still the Epiphany in mind, also elect a king by lot. Whenever he raises his glass to drink, others must follow.

Plough Monday Events
In 1980, after a lapse of 71 years, the tradition of a man dressing as a 'straw bear' was revived in the small Fenland town of Whittlesey near Peterborough. Now the 'bear' appears during the Plough Sunday weekend (usually following Plough Monday) when a big festival includes a souvenir stall at St Mary's selling 'I follow the bear' t-shirts and ends with a ceremonial burning of the straw bear costume.

The 2009 revival in Ramsey in Cambridgeshire has resulted in a straw bear leading pupils on Plough Monday lunchtime from the school to the site of the abbey opposite the church. Within living memory children used to go Plough Witching, which involved singing a rhyme door to door to collect money: 'I've a hole in my stocking and a hole in my shoe/Please give me a penny or two/if you ain't got a penny a halfpenny will do/ If you ain't got a halfpenny God bless you.' The bear figure resembles the Buttnmandl figures that accompany St Nicholas in Berchtesgaden every December and is a precursor of the similar bear which appears in a few weeks time at the Markina-Xemein carnival in Spain's Basque region.

Eaton Socon at St Neots in Cambridgeshire is among other places in East Anglia where Plough Monday customs have been revived to be kept on the traditional day. Here in the evening people gather for blessing the plough in front of the church before dancing outside The Waggon and Horses and The White Horse.

Mepal Molly Men dance at dusk in Ely Market Place.

The ploughman's song is sung this evening at ten locations around Balsham in Cambridgeshire since Plough Monday was revived in 1972.

This evening at Maldon in Essex, in a tradition claimed to date from 1522, a plough is moved from Hythe Quay and along the High Street to The Carpenters Arms by Morris dancers. The plough will have been taken to St Mary's Church last night to be blessed at the Epiphany carol service.

Grimsby Morris Men take part in a lantern procession and perform a plough play outside The Red Lion at Redbourne in Lincolnshire.

Plough Monday was the occasion when ploughing matches were held on the City of London's country estates and the Lord Mayor presided at a Grand Court of Wardmote to receive the returns for the local elections held on St Thomas's Day. This evening a Plow Monday service, a successor to the Plow Sunday service which the Lord Mayor used to attend in state, is held at St Lawrence Jewry. In 2010 the congregation held mobile phones in the air to be blessed as their tool in the coming year rather the plough. 'May our tongues be gentle, our e-mails be simple and our websites be accessible' were the words of one prayer.

The Lord Mayor hosts a Plow Monday dinner at Mansion House which has been held since at least the 18th century but is now an occasion to honour retiring Corporation staff. The Feltmakers' Company holds a Plough Monday dinner addressed, in a tradition started in 1936, by the two City Sheriffs.

UNITY WEEK

Week of Prayer for Christian Unity
18 to 25 January

The Week of Prayer for Christian Unity begins on 18 January and ends on the Conversion of St Paul, 25 January.

This special week towards the end of the Christmas period gives the opportunity to remember that when Christ founded the Church he warned that it should not be a divided body. Joint church events offer the chance to be with fellow Christians in other traditions who have also been celebrating Christmas and will shortly be keeping Lent and Easter.

Week of Prayer

The Week of Prayer was started in 1908 by two Anglican priests. Its origin can be traced to a sermon delivered on St Peter's Day 29 June 1900 at St Matthew's Westminster by Spencer Jones who was Vicar of Moreton-in-Marsh. Two years later the text was published as a book, *England and the Holy See*. Friar Paul Wattson, founder of the Franciscan Friars of the Atonement in Graymoor, New York State, read the book and began a correspondence with Fr Jones. In November 1907 the English priest proposed in a letter to his American colleague that St Peter's Day in June should be a day of prayer for unity. Fr Wattson's response suggested daily prayer for unity from the Feast of St Peter's Chair on 18 January to the Conversion of St Paul on 25 January. This was rapidly agreed for 1908. Pope Benedict XV extended its observance to the entire Church in 1916.

(In 1969 St Peter's Chair was moved to be combined with the similar feast of the Chair of St Peter on 22 February. The latter marked Peter becoming Bishop of Rome and the former Peter being consecrated Bishop of Antioch.)

A Split Church

The Orthodox Church was hived off from the Roman Catholic Church in 1054. In Britain the Church finally split during Elizabeth I's reign into Anglicans and exiled or underground Roman Catholics. Methodists, a group of Anglicans frustrated by a lack of mission, broke from the Church of England in 1744.

Steps to Unity

William Wake, Archbishop of Canterbury from 1716 to 1737, was the first Anglican primate after the Reformation to engage in dialogue with other churches and agree to intercommunion. In 1821 James Haldane Stewart, later rector of Limpsfield in Surrey, published *Hints for the General Union of Christians for the Outpouring of the Spirit* and from 1837 he advocated an annual day of prayer.

In 1840 George Spencer, a convert to Roman Catholicism who soon joined the Passionist order, suggested a 'Union of Prayer for Unity'.

In 1866 the Society of the Sisters of Bethany was founded with one of its main aims being to offer regular prayer for the visible reunion of the Church.

At the first Lambeth Conference the following year, Archbishop of Canterbury Charles Longley spoke of 'promoting the Reunion of Christendom'. His successor Archibald Tait maintained significant engagement with other churches and by 1868 the Association for Promoting the Unity of Christendom had 12,000 members.

In 1895 Leo XIII dedicated a novena of prayer for the 'Reunion of our separated brethren'. However, the following year, despite a Papal Commission narrowly favouring the recognition of Anglican orders, Pope Leo issued Apostolicae Curae declaring that 'ordinations carried out according to Anglican rites have been and are absolutely null and void'.

In 1910, two years after the Week of Prayer had been

established, the World Missionary Conference meeting at Edinburgh included a discussion about unity. One of the delegates was the Rev Dr Ching-yi Cheng, later the first General Secretary of the National Christian Council of China, who said: 'Speaking plainly we hope to see, in the near future, a united Christian Church without any denominational distinctions.'

There was another search for common ground in 1921 when Anglican Lord Halifax, churchwarden at St Mary's Bourne Street and a close collaborator of Spencer Jones, initiated a six year series of talks in Belgium between a group of Anglican priests and Cardinal Désiré Mercier of Malines. The following year Pius XI gave his blessing to the dialogue on his first full day as Pope although later he did not encourage inter-church meetings. Among those involved in the Malines Conversations over the next few years, until the Cardinal's death in 1926, were the Dean of Wells and Bishop Charles Gore. The spirit continues today as the ecumenical partnership between the Anglican Archdiocese of York, the Roman Catholic Diocese of Middlesborough and the Archdiocese of Mechelen-Brussels also known as Malines.

By 1932 the Church of England and the Old Catholics came to an agreement. Old Catholic orders are recognised by Rome and now most Anglicans can claim the Apostolic succession through members of the Old Catholic Church who have taken part in Anglican ordinations and consecrations.

By then the Fellowship of St Alban and St Sergius had been formed in London to foster Anglican-Orthodox relations. In 1935 Abbé Paul Couturier of France, inspired by meeting exiled Orthodox and learning about Cardinal Mercier's discussions with Anglicans, advocated the 'Universal Week of Prayer for Christian Unity' on the inclusive basis of prayer for 'the unity Christ wills by the means he wills'.

The phrase 'ecumenical movement' was introduced in 1941 by Archbishop of Canterbury William Temple. The World Council of Churches was formed in 1948. The Institute for Ecumenics at Paderborn was founded in 1957 and influenced Pope John XXIII.

The idea of summoning the Second Vatican Council came to Pope John during the 1959 Week of Prayer for Christian Unity and the announcement was made on the last day at St Paul Outside-the-Walls. The Pope wanted the Council to hasten unity and at Pentecost the next year he set up the Secretariat for Promoting Christian Unity (Pontifical Council from 1988) under Cardinal Augustin Bea. The secretary was the Johannes Willebrands who that year talked to Archbishop of Canterbury Geoffrey Fisher at a conference in St Andrews. In 1960 he was the first Archbishop of Canterbury since 1397 to visit a Pope.

At the opening of the Vatican Council in 1962 Pope John said: 'When we look back on history let us not try to seek to establish who was right and who was wrong. Responsibility is divided. Let us come together to try to put an end to our divisions, and seek in all things the will of Christ. We all need to be healed of memories in which we suffered, or caused others to suffer, in the name of Christ. We did it in the name of religion but not of Christ.' Exactly six years later Pope Paul VI came to address ecumenical observers at the end of the Council and expressed the hope that differences could be resolved 'slowly, gradually, loyally, generously'.

The Council's Decree on Ecumenicism affirmed that promoting unity between all Christians was one of the principal objectives of the Council. In 1964, the year the Vatican Council encouraged observance of the week of prayer, Pope Paul VI met Patriach Athenagoras I in Jerusalem. This was the first meeting between the leaders of the Roman Catholic and Orthodox Churches for over 500 years. They decided 'to cancel from the Church's memory the sentence of excommunication which had been pronounced' centuries earlier.

In 1966 the Anglican-Roman Catholic International Commission was set up and the Anglican Centre in Rome opened to facilitate contact between Canterbury and Rome. This followed a meeting in the Sistine Chapel between Pope Paul VI, who called the Anglican Church 'our well beloved sister', and Archbishop of Canterbury Michael Ramsey. When they said farewell, at St Paul

Outside-the-Walls, the Pope gave his ring to the Archbishop. It is worn by successor primates during their visits to Rome.

In 1970 Cardinal Willebrands, the new President of the Vatican's Secretariat for Christian Unity, suggested that the Anglican Communion should retain its traditions such as choral evensong and married clergy under any unity agreement.

In 1973 Paul VI and Pope Shenouda of the Coptic Church agreed to set up a commission following the return of some relics of St Mark to Alexandria.

Pope John Paul II's long reign saw an inexorable Anglican-Roman Catholic reconciliation despite the Church of England decision in 1992 to ordain women. A decade earlier he had visited Canterbury and asked Christians to continue the pilgrim journey together. At the time Archbishop Robert Runcie was hoping for unity as a 'uniate church' by the millennium year.

In 1995 His Holiness issued his encyclical *Ut Unum Sint* (That They May Be One) in which he recalled 'with profound emotion…praying… with the Primate of the Anglican Communion in Canterbury Cathedral'. He wrote of the need for constant reform of the church, of unity being an immense task which we cannot refuse, reviewing his own role as Bishop of Rome and the burning desire to join in celebrating one Eucharist of the Lord. The letter ended: 'Ecumenism is not only an internal question of the Christian Communities. It is a matter of the love which God has in Jesus Christ for all humanity; to stand in the way of this love is an offence against him and against his plan to gather all people in Christ.'

The following year the Pope and Archbishop of Canterbury George Carey co-presided at Vespers in St Gregorio al Celio where St Augustine had set out for England in 597. This has been repeated by successive Popes and Anglican Archbishops.

In 1999 Cardinal Edward Cassidy signed an agreement with the Lutherans on the doctrine of justification.

In Millennium Year 2000 the Pope invited the Anglican Archbishop of Canterbury and a representative of the Orthodox Ecumenical Patriarch to join him in opening the Holy Year Door at St Paul's-Outside-the-Walls on the first day of the Week of Prayer for Christian Unity. Later in the year Cardinal Cassidy, President of the Vatican's Pontifical Council for Promoting Christian Unity, told the Toronto meeting of Anglican and Roman Catholic bishops that the question of the the validity of Anglican orders 'is not something that says the orders are not valid or worth nothing'.

During the year the Pope said that the Roman Catholic Church 'suffers from the fact that true particular Churches and Ecclesial Communities with precious elements of salvation are separated from her'. In the autumn, when the Queen visited the Vatican, Pope John Paul said: 'There can be no turning back from the ecumenical goal we have set ourselves in obedience to the Lord's command.'

In 2001, when the present Anglican-Roman Catholic Working Group had its inaugural meeting, Pope John Paul said that full and visible unity will come 'as a divine gift at a time which we cannot know but for which we must prepare'.

In the late 20th century Methodist leader Donald Soper saw his church as one day being a preaching order in the Roman Catholic Church but in 1972 the expected union between Anglicans and Methodists failed to gain enough Anglican support. Thirty years later the Methodists and the Church of England General Synod agreed the Anglican-Methodist Covenant for discussion and in 2003 the International Methodist-Catholic Dialogue Commission began work in Rome. Meanwhile the Vatican continued its discussions with the Lutheran World Federation whose churches are now in communion with Anglicans.

In 2003 Cardinal Walter Kasper represented the Holy See at the enthronement of Archbishop Rowan Williams at Canterbury and afterwards presented the new primate with a pectoral cross from the Pope.

In 2004 Pope John Paul granted the ecumenical patriarchate use of the church of St Theodore on the Palatine Hill enabling the Greek-Orthodox archdiocese in Italy to have a significant and continuing presence close to the tomb of the Apostle Peter.

Pope Benedict XVI, in his first sermon, pledged to do all in his power 'to promote the fundamental cause of ecumenism' and within weeks designated St Paul Outside-the-Walls as a centre for Christian Unity gatherings. In 2006 Archbishop of Canterbury Rowan Williams celebrated the Eucharist in the Church of Santa Sabina in Rome.

Pope Francis, soon after his election, said: 'We must walk united with our differences: there is no other way to become one. This is the way of Jesus.' In 2016 he visited the Lutheran Church in Sweden at the start of the Luther anniversary year. 'The intention of Martin Luther five hundred years ago was to renew the Church, not divide her,' said the Pope.

In The Bible

John 17.20-21 and I Corinthians 12.12

At the Last Supper Jesus prayed for those who will come to believe in him: 'May they all be one.' This was the beginning of the church. St Paul, writing to the Corinthians said: 'For as with the human body which is a unity although it has many parts – all the parts of the body, though many, still making up one single body – so it is with Christ.'

In Church

A prayer for unity is included in daily services and on the Sunday, sometimes called Christian Unity Sunday, it is not unusual for the pulpit to be occupied by a preacher from another denomination. Often one church will host a special service on a weekday during the week.

A popular hymn for these services is *The Church's one foundation* written in 1866 by S. J. Stone when he was curate at Windsor parish church. It was inspired by a bitter internal Anglican dispute between the Archbishop of Cape Town and the Bishop of Natal. The original tune is Aurelia, composed by SS Wesley just two years earlier at Winchester Cathedral for the hymn *Jerusalem the golden*. Stone, who added little-known verses for processional use, later became Vicar of St Paul's Haggerston and Rector of All Hallows-on-the-Wall in the City of London.

Week of Prayer Events

In London the choir of the Roman Catholic Westminster Cathedral sings Vespers at Anglican St Paul's Cathedral on one day during the week and on another the choir of St Paul's sings evensong at Westminster Cathedral.

The Sisters of Bethany, now at Southsea, hold an act of worship with a speaker on (usually) the Wednesday in the week.

On the concluding day, the feast of the Conversion of St Paul, there is an ecumenical gathering with the Pope for Vespers at Rome's St Paul Outside-the-Walls.

St Henry of Finland
19 January

St Henry, English-born patron saint of Finland, was appointed Bishop of Uppsala in 1152. He was consecrated bishop by Englishman Nicholas Breakspear who later became Pope Hadrian IV. Henry accompanied the King of Sweden St Eric on a visit to Finland where they faced hostility but Henry stayed on as a missionary. In about 1156 he was killed with an axe by a man he had condemned for murdering a Swedish soldier.

Henry was buried at Nousis and in 1300 the body was moved to Turku. His relics are now in the care of a museum but a bone is embedded in the main altar of St Henry's Roman Catholic Cathedral in Helsinki.

Today, the second day of the Week of Prayer for Christian Unity, is an occasion for Finnish dialogue between Lutherans and Roman Catholics. By a tradition started in 1989, the Pope receives an ecumenical delegation of Finnish clergy.

St Agnes' Day
21 January

St Agnes' Day is probably best known for John Keats' poem 'The Eve of St Agnes'. This was written in 1819 when, especially in Yorkshire, it was still the tradition on the evening of 20 January for young ladies to pray and eat special food in the hope of seeing their future husband in a dream. In 1637 Van Dyck painted the soon to be married Lady Mary Villiers holding a palm and a lamb, symbols of martyr St Agnes. Alfred Tennyson also wrote a poem called 'St Agnes' Eve' and Pre-Raphaelite painters William Holman Hunt, John Millais and Arthur Hughes all depicted Keats' poem. Holman Hunt's even includes a little holly left over from Christmas. Stained glass artist Harry Clarke is best known for his 1924 'Eve of St Agnes' double window in Dublin. 'Saint Agnes' fountain' features in the carol Good King Wenceslas (see page 90).

St Agnes

Agnes was a 13 year old girl put to death with a sword in Rome by the Romans in about 304. She was consigned to a brothel for refusing the sexual advances and proposal of a young Roman prefect and preferred having her throat cut to losing her virginity. Her name has been remembered today since 366 and was, like St Lucy (see page 48), included in the canon of the Mass.

The Church of St Agnes at the Circus (Sant Agnese in Agone) in Piazza Navona covers the site of the brothel where she was murdered and her skull is there in the front of an altar. A marble relief shows her with the long hair said to have suddenly grown to cover part of her exposed body. Another church, St

Agnes Outside the Walls (Sant Agnese Fuori le Mura) on the Via Nomentana, is built over her tomb and holds her body.

Agnes is the patron saint of young girls, chastity and survivors of sexual assault..

Other St Agnes Churches

There are several churches in England dedicated to Agnes including the 14th-century landmark church at Cawston in Norfolk, the small but lavish church at Newmarket built in 1885, the also Victorian St Agnes at Kennington in London which was rebuilt after war damage, the City of London's St Anne and St Agnes (a unique double dedication) which for 45 years until 2013 had a Lutheran congregation, the huge St Agnes Toxteth in Liverpool designed by John Loughbrough Pearson which opened in 1885 and the thatched St Agnes at Freshwater Bay on the Isle of Wight built in 1908 on land given by Tennyson's eldest son and dedicated to Agnes at the suggestion of his wife. St Agnes near Grand Central Terminal in New York, one of the city's busiest churches, was rebuilt in the 1990s as a smaller version of Rome's Church of the Gesù following a huge fire.

Sheep and Archbishops

The similarity between Agnes and *agnus* meaning lamb has led to an association with lambs. St Agnes is depicted with sheep in the 6th-century mosaics in Ravenna and in Keats' poem there is mention of St Agnes and her lambs unshorn and the flock in woolly fold.

Today the Pope blesses two lambs less than year old whose wool will be used to make the pallium given to each new metropolitan archbishop, one who heads a province or group of dioceses. The lambs are reared by Rome's convent of San Lorenzo in Panisperna and, in a tradition dating from 1884, spent last night in the laundry room at the nearby Sisters of the Holy Family of Nazareth in the Via Machiavelli. Today the two are taken in flower decorated baskets to St Agnes Outside the Walls where during the 10am Mass they are placed on the altar over the Agnes' tomb and blessed. Each has a floral wreath on their head: one red to recall martyrdom and the other white for virginity. The long custom has been for the lambs to then go to the Vatican for the Papal blessing. However, Pope Francis has been known to bless the lambs after his 8am Mass before their visit to St Agnes Outside the Walls. Finally they go to the Santa Cecilia convent in Trastevere. Appropriately, the convent's early 8th-century church apse mosaic depicts lambs. There at Easter the two lambs will be shorn for their wool. 'Only two will be enough to make them all?' asked Pope Francis when he first carried out the ceremony. Vatican officials had no answer but the nuns always mix the lamb's wool with other wool for the making of each pallium which vary in number year by year.

The pallium is a Y shaped loose collar worn over the chasuble at Mass on special occasions by an archbishop in his own diocese. The design includes five crosses representing Christ's five wounds received at the crucifixion and three nails representing the nails which were driven through Christ's hands and crossed feet. This addition to the vestments is the symbol of the jurisdiction that only the Pope can give an archbishop. The conferral of the pallium renews the unity of each group of dioceses with the Apostolic See and the successor to St Peter.

But the pallium, dating from the 4th century, is also an important symbol of the Pope's and an archbishop's association with the martyrs of Rome. Archbishops are to be in the words of St Peter (1 Peter 5:3) 'examples to the flock'. The pallium symbolises the sheep on the shoulders of Jesus the Good Shepherd.

On the eve of the feast of St Peter and St Paul (29 June) each pallium is placed in a niche near St Peter's tomb in the Vatican basilica and given to new archbishops the following day after the Papal Mass.

In this Week of Prayer for Christian Unity it is interesting to note that Pope John Paul II said of those who wear the pallium: 'They are thus called to take a leading role in building up the Church's unity, which is expressed in the profession of the one faith and in fraternal charity.' Although Anglican archbishops do not receive the pallium it is depicted on the Archbishop of Canterbury's coat of arms used on official documents.

If today is a Wednesday then the Pope will probably bless the lambs at the close of the General Audience in the Pope Paul VI Hall before the visitors depart. However, when 21 January falls on a Sunday then the blessing of the lambs is held on the Saturday.

In Church
The RC Eucharistic Prayer 1 includes mention of St Agnes.

Today at St Agnes' Tomb
At St Agnes Outside the Walls there is a parish Mass in the evening in addition to the morning celebration with the lambs.

Other St Agnes Celebrations
At St Agnes Church, in London's Kennington, relics are placed on the altar and a statue is decorated with flowers for an evening Mass if today is a weekday.

At Liverpool's St Agnes, Toxteth Park the main Mass in the evening includes a procession with a relic.

The hill village of Sainte-Agnès above Menton in the south of France has street dancing and singing.

The sixth Mass of the day (5.10pm) at New York's St Agnes Church is a Solemn Mass in honour of the patron.

END OF CHRISTMAS

Candlemas

2 February

The feast of the Presentation of the Lord comes forty days after Christmas Day and is commonly called Candlemas since candles, representing Jesus the 'light to lighten the pagans', play an important role in today's Mass.

Candlemas is the end of the Christmas period, or the fulfilment of Christmas, celebrating six week old Baby Jesus leaving Bethlehem and being presented at the Temple in Jerusalem thirty-three days after his circumcision (Leviticus 12.1-4). This is one of the ancient holy days which has been observed in England since at least the early 10th century.

It is the celebration of Jesus Christ, Light of the Nations. Just as Advent began with candles held during an Advent carol service (see page 18) so again lighted candles are held at the very end of the season as a welcome to Christ who has been brought to us.

Candlemas is a transitional feast with its recognition of Holy Week to come from Simeon's words that greet Jesus in the Temple. The procession into the main church is a foretaste of the Palm Sunday procession which will represent the adult Christ entering Jerusalem and the Temple. The verses in today's responsorial psalm will again be heard when sung during the Psalm Sunday procession.

At the entrance to the Temple, Mary and Joseph would have bought the two pigeons from one of the stalls that Jesus was to overturn following his entry on the first Palm Sunday.

In the middle ages, when the new Easter candle was also blessed today, it was easier to look ahead beyond Lent to when

Christ rising from the dead would be celebrated on Easter Day. On Candlemas 1247 Henry III gave 1000lbs of beeswax to Westminster Abbey for the making of a giant candle.

The link to Lent is even more real when it follows quickly as in 2008 when Shrove Tuesday came just three days afterwards on 5 February. In such years pre-Lent carnival abroad will already have begun and Candlemas will indeed be part of the preparation for Lent, Good Friday and Easter.

An old Candlemas Eve carol, 'Down with the Rosemary and Bays' by Robert Herrick (1591-1674), speaks in the second verse of taking down the decorations and looking ahead to Easter:

> *The holly hitherto did sway:*
> *Let now box domineer*
> *Until the dancing Easter day,*
> *Or Easter's eve appear.*

After today the crib and any remaining Christmas trees are removed from the church.

Development of Candlemas

The first record of this festival is in Jerusalem during the 4th century when it was observed with great joy on 14 February, forty days after Epiphany (see page 123). Pope Gelasius introduced the feast day to Rome in 492. About 688 Pope Sergius I added the candle procession which took place in darkness outdoors just before early morning Mass at Santa Maria Maggiore in Rome. Hence the name 'Candlemas' meaning Candle Mass or a Mass where candles featured more than at other Masses. In time it became the day when the stock of candles for the coming year was blessed.

By the 10th century it was known in the West as the Purification of the Blessed Virgin Mary and observed as now on 2 February. 'Purification' was inspired by St Luke's account where he records as one event Mary being ritually purified after childbirth (Leviticus 12:2-8) and presenting her first born male at the Temple.

However, the title Purification of the Blessed Virgin Mary tended to suggest that today was a festival of Mary when it is a festival of the Lord and really an extension of Epiphany. The Roman Catholic Church changed the name in 1969 to the Presentation of the Lord. In the Eastern Orthodox Church today is known as the Meeting of the Lord or the Feast of Meeting.

Although today is an important feast it is not a day of obligation and so tends to be forgotten by many. But in some places it remains a turning point in the agricultural year with cattle removed from a common so that the hay crop can be grown ready for cutting before Lammas Day on 1 August in six months' time.

The wedding of James I of Scotland to Englishwoman Joan at Southwark Cathedral in 1423 took place at Candlemas. In 1514 Henry VIII chose today to create two new Dukes and two new Earls at a ceremony in Lambeth Palace which was preceded by Mass in the chapel. Charles I's coronation was today in 1626. Several City livery companies, including the Grocers' and Horners', hold their annual service today reminding us of how Candlemas was in the past considered to be an important a day. Today is a red letter day in the law calendar when High Court judges can wear a scarlet robe.

The first performance of Shakespeare's *Twelfth Night* in 1602 was not at Epiphany but at a Candlemas feast attended by law students in the Middle Temple Hall.

What Happened Today
Luke 2.22-38

Joseph and Mary followed the Jewish law by taking their first born male Jesus from Bethlehem to the Temple at Jerusalem, about an hour's uphill walk, to be presented to the Lord. The incident parallels the account in the Old Testament of Hannah presenting her baby Samuel at the temple of Yahweh at Shiloh and meeting Eli (1 Samuel 1:24-28).

The purchase at the Temple entrance of two pigeons for sacrifice by the poor parents, who could not afford a lamb, was part of the purification of Mary. (Joseph may also have obtained the customary five shekels for the child's redemption on presentation.) Inside the Temple, to Mary and Joseph's surprise, an old man called Simeon was waiting for them having been prompted by the Holy Spirit to go to the there. Simeon, who had believed that he would see Christ before he died, took the Christ Child in his arms and uttered the words we now hear at Evening Prayer and know as the Nunc Dimittis: 'Now, Master, you are letting your servant go in peace as you promised; for my eyes have seen the salvation which you have made ready in the sight of the nations; a light of revelation for the gentiles and the glory for your people Israel.'

Simeon then blessed the Holy Family and turning to Mary warned of the difficult times which lay thirty years ahead during Jesus' ministry and final days on earth: 'Look, he is destined for the fall and the rise of many in Israel, destined to be a sign that is opposed – and a sword will pierce your soul too – so that the secret thoughts of many may be laid bare.'

Anna, an 84 year old widow who spent all day every day fasting and praying in the Temple, passed by and recognised Jesus as the Messiah. Elderly Simeon and Anna represent the years of waiting for Christ to appear.

After this traumatic and moving encounter, the Holy Family returned, maybe via Egypt (see page 96), to Nazareth where Jesus was to grow up quietly.

In Church

The main Mass today begins with the blessing of candles and a procession of all the congregation and clergy holding lighted candles to symbolise the realisation of Simeon's prophecy of a light for the gentiles. If possible the congregation should meet in a side chapel, or an adjoining building, for the blessing of candles and sprinkling. Then everyone follows the celebrant into the church to welcome Christ.

The lighted procession entering the main church, to the singing of Simeon's Nunc Dimittis song, can also represent the entrance of the True Light, the Christ Child, into the Temple. The congregation goes into the 'Temple' to greet the Lord who each person is about to meet in the sacrament of Holy Communion.

It would not be inappropriate to follow the medieval custom of taking the Baby from the crib and carrying the Christ Child figure in the candle procession. If it is evening the church should be in darkness.

Where there cannot be a procession of all the people, candles are distributed to the congregation. The celebrant and serving party form a small procession after blessing the candles from the back of the church.

The Mass begins with the Gloria. Once candles would have been lit and extinguished for the procession, Gospel and prayer of consecration. Now members of the congregation are free to keep their candle alight as long as they wish – maybe until the Gospel or, if not receiving Communion, even throughout the Mass. But often a priest will say 'please extinguish your candles' at an appropriate point such as just before the readings or at the sermon. In St Peter's in Rome the candles are extinguished after the collect and as the electric light is turned up for the readings.

The Old Testament reading from the Book of Malachi (written about 460 BC) includes the foretelling of the Presentation: '... the Lord whom you are seeking will come and enter his Temple'. The Gospel reading is Luke's description of the Presentation and is one of the longest accounts of the infancy of Christ.

Some Anglican churches, using Common Worship, hold the procession at the end of the Mass with the Nunc Dimittis being sung. A procession after the Mass, out of the main church, can represent the Holy Family going home to Nazareth, maybe by way of Egypt (see page 96).

The liturgical colour is white but just as priests used to wear purple vestments for the procession before mass so purple can be worn when the procession is at the end as the colour provides a link to coming Lent when penitential purple will be the daily colour.

Some churches have a display of unlit new candles for use in the coming year and these are blessed at the start of Mass.

Suitable hymns are *Hail to the Lord who comes* and *Lead, kindly light*.

It is traditional to have snowdrops, known as Candlemas Bells, decorating the church.

Other Candlemas Celebrations

At Blidworth in Nottinghamshire, on the first Sunday in February, the Rocking Ceremony is held at 3pm in the church which is dedicated to St Mary of the Purification. A male child, one born nearest Christmas Day, is baptised in the morning and brought back to church by his parents and godparents. During the service a Bible for the child is blessed and presented to the parents at the altar. The priest, usually a visiting bishop or archdeacon, places the child in an 18th-century wooden cradle covered with flowers. This is gently rocked by the priest as the congregation says the General Thanksgiving. After the child has been handed back, the Nunc Dimittus is sung. This custom, once more widespread especially in churches with the same dedication, was recorded here in the form of a short play in the 13th century when Maid Marian lived in the village. It lapsed in about 1690 and was first revived in 1842 and, after another break, in 1922. Blidworth Church, in the centre of Sherwood Forest and burial place of Robin Hood's Will Scarlet, has a memorial to forest ranger Thomas Leake who died on 4 February 1608 after a Candlemas drinking bout led to a fatal fight. Two windows, including the east window, depict the Presentation. The 1936 Rocking Baby Ray Harris later became churchwarden. Since 2010 there has been a cradle sculpture, designed and made by Morris Reddington, in the main street.

A Festal Mass in Ripon Cathedral features over 4,000 candles. Some are used to make decorations and others carried in procession by the congregation. This show of candles survived the Reformation and continued until the end of the 18th century. In 1790 the building was described being 'one continued blaze of light all afternoon'. The custom was revived in the late 20th century and now attracts a congregation of around 600.

In Marseille, in southern France, there is a very well-attended pre-dawn Mass at St Victor's Abbey in Marseille at 6.15am which is in keeping with the earliest tradition of today. The vestments and candles are green to symbolise spring shoots.

Much earlier, at 5am, a 13th-century statue of the Virgin Mary is brought up from the crypt for an outdoor procession during which the Gospels are collected from a vessel in the harbour. At 6am, on a viewpoint by Rue Neuve Sainte-Catherine outside St Victor's, there is the blessing of green candles and Marseilles.

After the Mass, at 8am, there is a blessing and sharing of Navettes, local Candlemas biscuits once distributed by the Abbey, at the nearby Le Four des Navettes bakery where they have been sold loose since 1781. The seven inch long hard biscuit, with a distinctive aroma and a slight orange taste, has a slash down the middle indicating a boat to recall the legend of Lazarus, Mary Magdalene and Martha arriving on the coast. Relics of Mary Magdalene, the first to discover the Resurrection, are thirty miles away at Saint Maximin-la-Sainte-Baume. Some of Lazarus's now lost relics were brought to Marseilles in the early 13th century when the shrine of St Victor was a major pilgrimage destination. Elsewhere in France pancakes are often eaten today as they will soon be in England on the eve of Lent.

Christmas to Lent

During Christmas there are reminders of the eventual outcome of the Christmas story. Christmas celebrations can only be justified because it is known that the Baby is the son of God who was rejected and killed before rising and ascending.

The Holy Thorn of Glastonbury blossom on the Queen's Christmas lunch table, often still blooming at Candlemas, is said to be derived from the staff of Joseph of Arimathea who took Christ's body down from the Cross. Indeed it is claimed to be of the same thorn as the Crown of Thorns worn by Christ just before his crucifixion. The holly sprig stuck in the pudding has red berries said to be a reminder of the crown of thorns and blood.

The Three Kings looked to that time by bringing myrrh as a symbol of Christ's death on Good Friday. On Epiphany night Cologne Cathedral is warm with candles and above the high altar there is the huge golden casket containing the remains of the Magi. But the reliquary's fine decoration includes Christ on the Cross. Walk behind to the Chapel of the Three Kings and you will find the shadow of a small cross, which hangs above its entrance, dramatically magnified across the windows and wall by the light from the shrine. The Christmas glow throws up the unavoidable shadow of the Cross.

During Lent which follows sooner or later after Candlemas there is time to think about the enormity of the true story of Christmas.

APPENDICES

CHRISTMAS CAROLS

Wynkyn de Worde, who had a printing press by St Bride's Church in Fleet Street published carols in 1521. They tended to be in English rather than the Latin of public worship. The suppression of carols by the Puritans in the 16th century meant that by the beginning of Queen Victoria's reign *God rest ye merry gentlemen* was one of the few carols known to most people. However, medieval carols were still being sung at Oxford Colleges and in 1871 Magdalen College fellow Henry Bramley and composer John Stainer, who was Magdalen organist, edited *Christmas Carols Old and New* which introduced *The first Nowell*.

In 1901 George Woodward, Vicar of Walsingham, published *The Cowley Carol Book* which included his own carol *Ding-dong! Merrily on High!* and in 1928 *The Oxford Book of Carols* contributed to the growth of carol services. This was the same year that the Nine Lessons and Carols service was first broadcast from King's College, Cambridge on Christmas Eve.

Other Carols

Angels from the realms of glory by James Montgomery first appeared in the *Sheffield Advertiser* on Christmas Eve 1816.

Away in a manger, by an unknown author, first appeared in 1885 in the *Little Children's Book for Schools and Families* published by the Lutheran Church in North America. The familiar music was added ten years later by William James Kirkpatrick, Director of Music at Grace Church in Philadelphia.

Christians, awake, salute the happy morn was written as a poem for Christmas 1745 by shorthand inventor John Byrom (1692-1763) who originated the epigram Tweedledee and Tweedledum for a disagreement between composers. It has been claimed that Byrom wrote the poem at Jackson's Boat, a pub by the River Mersey in Sale. The tune was composed in 1750 by his friend John Wainwright.

Gloomy night embraced the place is a song of the shepherds by poet Richard Crashaw (1612-1650) who is buried at Loreto. The tune is an Alsatian cradle song.

Hark! The herald Angels sing was written by Charles Wesley in 1760 and set to a tune first heard at Drury Lane Theatre in 1715 when the opera *Venus and Adonis* was performed. Later the words were improved by Dr William Cummings, organist at Waltham Abbey, who used Mendelssohn's 1840 cantata written to celebrate the 400th anniversary of the printing press. Today's familiar words and tune were heard first by a congregation at the Abbey church on Christmas Day 1855.

I saw three ships, derived from the idea of the Three Kings bodies arriving by river at Cologne, originated in Newcastle-upon-Tyne in the 1830s.

In the bleak midwinter is a Christmas poem written in 1872 by Christina Rossetti for a magazine and, a decade after her death, put to music in 1906 by Gustav Holst. It was first heard in Christ Church in Albany Street, London where the author attended. An alternative but little used tune was composed by Harold Darke in December 1909. The carol, and its original tune, was voted the nation's favourite carol in 2001 in a Classic FM poll.

Lully, lulla, thou little tiny child was probably written by Robert Croo about 1534 for the Coventry Corpus Christi play.

New Prince New Pomp, which begins *Behold a silly, tender babe,* was written during Elizabeth I's reign, possibly for persecuted English Roman Catholics, by St Robert Southwell who was executed in 1595.

O Christmas Tree, a German carol dating from 1824 by Ernest Anschutz, is sung to a German folk tune which was later adopted for *The Red Flag* sung at Labour Party conferences.

O come, all ye faithful, better known abroad in its original Latin *Adeste Fideles*, appeared about 1750 according to a manuscript at Stoneyhurst College. The English version dating from 1841 was written by Frederick Oakley who was first curate at Anglican All Saints Margaret Street, when it was known as the Margaret Chapel, and then a priest at St George's Roman Catholic Cathedral, then just a parish church, in Southwark.

O Holy Night was written in 1847 by French wine merchant Placide Cappeau and days later was sung at midnight Mass at Roquemaure. It was translated into English by John Sullivan Dwight. The tune is by Adolphe-Charles Adam who composed the ballet *Giselle*.

O little town of Bethlehem was written in 1867 by the Revd Philip Brooks two years after he had ridden from Jerusalem to Bethlehem on a donkey.

Once in royal David's city, written by Fanny Humphreys (Mrs Alexander) before her marriage to a future Anglican Archbishop of Armagh, appeared as a poem in 1848 and was set to music by H. J. Gauntlett the following year.

See amid the winter snow was written in 1851 by Edward Caswall whilst a priest and colleague of Blessed John Henry Newman at The Oratory in Edgbaston. As an Anglican Fr Caswall had been perpetual curate at St Lawrence's Stratford-sub-Castle near Salisbury.

Silent night, holy night was written in 1816 for guitar and two male voices by parish priest Joseph Mohr when curate at Arnsdorf in Austria. In 1818 Franz-Xaver Gruber, parish priest at St Nikolaus in Oberndorf on the Austrian-German border near Salzburg, arranged the music for several instruments after it was allegedly discovered, shortly before midnight Mass, that mice had nibbled the organ bellows. The German carol was still largely unknown in Britain a century later. However, when British troops on Christmas Eve 1914 heard Germans across the lines singing *Stille Nacht* they instantly knew it was a carol and responded with *A first Nowell* followed eventually by *Adeste Fidelis*. Since 1818 *Silent night* has been translated into 320 languages. A chapel stands on the site of the Oberndorf church which was demolished following flood damage. On Christmas Eve it is sung hourly from 5pm on Austrian television by the Vienna Boys' Choir. In Austria it is never sung in Advent or any other day during Christmas.

The holly and the ivy was first sung in the 18th century and saved for a wider audience by Cecil Sharp who heard it in Gloucestershire and recorded the words and tune.

We three kings of Orient are, by Pennsylvanian parish priest and future bishop John Henry Hopkins, was written in 1857 for a college Christmas pageant in New York and published in England in 1871.

While shepherds watched first appeared in 1700 having been written Nahum Tate who based it on Luke 2.8-14. With no known carols after the long Puritan years it became the popular Christmas hymn. The present tune by Handel was only adopted in 1861. The hymn writer became Poet Laureate under William III but was sacked when George I succeeded. Tate died in the Royal Mint hiding from his creditors and was buried in St George the Martyr churchyard in Southwark.

Regional Carols

A carol service, featuring old Dorset carols, is held on the Second Sunday in Advent at Bloxworth in Dorset at 3pm. The church is lit by over 50 candles and the music is provided by a small string orchestra. The carols were being sung door to door at the beginning of Queen Victoria's reign and then at the rectory from 1880 until the carol service was established in the 20th century. The collection of carols was compiled by William Pickard-Cambridge, whose father Octavious was Rector from 1868 to 1916, and parish clerk John Skinner. A total of 42 were published in 1926 along with details their place of origin in the Piddle Valley or on the Isle of Purbeck.

At Padstow, in Cornwall, local carols dating from at least the 18th century are sung outdoors from early December to Epiphany.

BIBLIOGRAPHY

Ackroyd, Peter, *Shakespeare: The Biography*, Chatto & Windus, 2005.

Allison, Ronald and Riddell, Sarah, *The Royal Encyclopedia*, Macmillan, 1991.

Arnold-Forster, Frances, *Studies in Church Dedications*, Skeffington, 1899.

Baker, Margaret, *Discovering Christmas Customs and Folklore*, Shire, 1992.

Baldwin, David, *The Chapel Royal: Ancient and Modern*, Duckworth, 1990.

Barron, Caroline and Saul, Nigel, *England and The Low Countries in the Late Middle Ages*, Sutton, 1995.

Baxter, Philip, *Sarum Use*, Sarum Script, 1994.

Beaton, Katherine, *The Real Santa Claus*, H&B Publications, 1986.

Beeson, Trevor, *Window on Westminster*, SCM Press, 1998.

Bertram, Anthony, *Paul Nash*, Faber, 1955.

Blair, John, *The Church in Anglo-Saxon Society*, Oxford, 2005.

Bogle, Joanna, *A Book of Feasts and Seasons*, Gracewing, 1988.

Bowker, John, *The Complete Bible Handbook*, Dorling Kindersley, 1998.

Bradley, Ian, *Pilgrimage: A Spiritual and Cultural Journey*, Lion, 2009.

Bradley, Ian, *The Penguin Book of Carols*, Penguin, 1999.

Bradley, Ian, *The Penguin Book of Hymns*, Penguin, 1990.

Bradshaw, Paul F. and Johnson Maxwell E., *The Origins of Feasts, Fasts and Seasons in Early Christianity*, SPCK, 2011.

Brown, David, *Tradition and Imagination*, Oxford, 1999.

Brown, H. Miles, *The Story of Truro Cathedral*, Tor Mark Press, 1991.

Carey, George, *The Bible for Everyday Life*, Lion, 2000.

Chandler, Andrew and Hein, David, *Archbishop Fisher 1945-1961: Church, State and World*, Ashgate, 2012.

Clarke, John, *Church Services for the Farming Year*, National Agricultural Centre, 1988.

Connelly, Mark, *Christmas: A Social History*, I.B. Tauris, 1999.

Cooke, Gillian, *A Celebration of Christmas*, Queen Anne Press, 1980.

Cooper, Quentin and Sullivan, Paul, *Maypoles, Martyrs and Mayhem*, Bloomsbury, 1994.

Cottiaux, Jean, *Sainte Julienne de Cornillon*, Carmel de Cornillon, 1991.

Davidson, Linda Kay and Gititz, David M., *Pilgrimage*, ABC-CLIO, 2002.

Drake-Carnell, F.J., *Old English Customs and Ceremonies*, Batsford, 1938.

Duffy, Eamon, *The Stripping of the Altars*, Yale, 1992.

Edwards, William Peterson, *The Festival of Nine Lessons and Carols*, Universe, 2004.

Farmer, David Hugh, *Oxford Dictionary of Saints*, OUP, 1987

Fass, Serena, *The Magi: Their Journey and their Contemporaries*, Chesil Court, 2015.

Fenton, J.C., *The Gospel According to John*, Oxford, 1970.

Fenton, J.C., *St Matthew*, Pelican, 1963.

Ferguson, James, *The Emmerdale Book of Country Lore*, Hamlyn, 1988.

Field, John, *Place-Names of Greater London*, Batsford, 1980.

Galbiati, Enrico, *The Gospel of Jesus*, Vicenza, Instituto S. Gaetiano, 1970.

Gaeta, Francis X, *Come—Celebrate Jesus!*, Resurrection Press New York, 1997.

Gant, Andrew, *Christmas Carols from Village Green to Church Choir*, Profile Books, 2014.

Gascoigne, Margaret, *Discovering English Customs and Traditions*, Shire, 1969.

Goddard, Philip J., *Festa Paschalia*, Gracewing, 2012.

Golby, J. M. and Purdue, A. W., *The Making of the Modern Christmas*, Sutton 2000.

Guarita, Carlos, *Theatre of the Seasons*, Lisboa Camara Municipal, 1999.

Guy, John, *Thomas Becket: Warrior, Priest, Rebel, Victim: A 900-Year-Old Story Retold*, Viking, 2012.

Hall, Ursula, *The Cross of St Andrew*, Birlinn, 2006.

Haffner, Paul, *The Mystery of Mary*, Gracewing, 2004.

Harrison, Frederick, *Medieval Man and His Notions*, John Murray, 1947.

Harrowven, Jean, *Origins of Festivals and Feasts*, Pryor, 1980.

Hartman, Tom, *Guinness Book of Christmas*, Guinness Superlatives, 1984.

Hole, Christina, *A Dictionary of British Folk Customs*, Paladin, 1987.

Hole, Christina, *Easter and Its Customs*, Richard Bell, 1961.

Hole, Christina, *English Traditional Customs*, Batsford, 1975.

Idle, Christopher, *Christmas Carols and Their Stories*, Lion, 1988.

Knightly, Charles, *The Customs and Ceremonies of Britain*, Thames & Hudson, 1986.

Lambarde, William, *Alphabetical Description of Chief Places in England and Wales*, 1730.

le Vay, Benedict, *Eccentric Britain*, Bradt, 2000.

Leeming, Bernard, *The Churches and the Church*, DLT, 1963.

Livingstone, E.A., *Concise Dictionary of the Christian Church*, Oxford, 1977.

Long, George, *The Folklore Calendar*, Senate, 1930.

Longford, Lord, *The Life of Jesus Christ*, Sidgwick & Jackson, 1974.

Marini, Piero, *A Challenging Reform: Realizing the Vision of the Liturgical Renewal, 1963-1975*, Liturgical Press, 2008.

Mackenzie, Neil, *The Medieval Boy Bishops*, Matador, 2012.

Martin, Elizabeth, *Sandwich Almshouses 1190-1975*, Sandwich Local History Society, 1974.

Mathews, Wendy, *My Ward*, Walpole House, 2009.

McArthur, A. Allan, *The Evolution of the Christian Year*, SCM, 1953.

Metford, J.C.J., *The Christian Year*, Thames & Hudson, 1991.

Muir, Frank, *Christmas Customs and Traditions*, Sphere, 1975.

Mulder-Bakker, Anneke B., *Living Saints of the Thirteenth Century*, Brepols, 2011.

Musto, Walter, *The War and Uncle Walter*, Bantam, 2004.

Nissenbaum, Stephen, *The Battle For Christmas*, Vintage Books USA, 1997.

Oldfield, Paul, *Sanctity and Pilgrimage in Medieval Southern Italy, 1000-1200*, Cambridge, 2014.

Orme, Nicholas, *Exeter Cathedral: The First Thousand Years, 400-1550*, Impress, 2009.

Palmer, Geoffrey and Lloyd, Noel, *A Year of Festivals*, Warne, 1972.

Palmer, Roy, *Britain's Living Folklore*, David & Charles, 1991.

Palmer, Roy, *The Folklore of Radnorshire*, Logaston Press, 2001.

Perham, Michael, *Celebrate the Christian Story*, SPCK, 1997.

Perham, Michael, *Liturgy Pastoral And Parochial*, SPCK, 1996.

Ratzinger, Joseph (Benedict XVI), *Jesus of Nazareth: The Infancy Narratives*, Bloomsbury, 2012.

Reid, Alcuin, *The Organic Development of the Liturgy*, Saint Michael's Abbey Press, 2004.

Rosenthal, J. M., 'Saint Nicholas', *Anglican World*, number 95 supplement, 1999.

Ryan, Vincent, *Advent to Epiphany*, Veritas, 1983.

Simpson, Jaqueline and Round, Steve, *A Dictionary of English Folklore*, Oxford, 2000.

Snell, F.J., *The Customs of Old England*, Methuen, 1911.

Sox, David, *Relics and Shrines*, Allen & Unwin, 1985.

Stanford, Caroline, *Dearest Augustus and I: The Journal of Jane Pugin*, Spire, 2004.

Sruthers, Jane, *The Book of Christmas*, Ebury Press, 2012.

Sykes, Homer, *Once a Year*, Gordon Fraser, 1977.

Symonds, Richard, *Diary of the Marches of the Royal Army*, Cambridge, 1998.

Tajani, Angelo, *Siracusa e Stoccolma*, Italconsult, 2005.

Tasker, R.V.G., *St Matthew*, Tyndale, 1961.

Tatton-Brown, Tim, *Lambeth Palace*, SPCK, 2000.

Tavinor, Michael, *Shrines of the Saints in England and Wales*, Canterbury, 2016.

Urlin, Ethel L., *Festivals, Holy Days and Saints' Days: A Study in Origins and Survivals in Church Ceremonies and Secular Customs*, Simpkin, Marshall, Hamilton, Kent, 1915.

Vermes, Geza, *The Nativity: History and Legend*, Penguin, 2006.

Vipont, Elfrida, *Some Christian Festivals*, Michael Joseph, 1963.

Walsh, Michael, *The* Universe *Book of Saints*, Geoffrey Chapman, 1994.

Wareham, Norman and Gill, Jill, *Every Pilgrim's Guide to the Holy Land*, Canterbury, 1998.

Weightman, Gavin and Humphries, Steve, *Christmas Past*, Sidgwick & Jackson, 1987.

Weinreb, Ben and Hibbert, Christopher, *Encyclopaedia of London*, Macmillan, 1983.

Whistler, Laurence, *The English Festivals*, Heinemann, 1947.

Willcocks, David, *Christmas Carols*, Sphere, 1975.

Wilson, Jan, *Feasting for Festivals*, Sandy Lane Books, 1990.

Yates, Nigel, *Anglican Ritualism in Victorian Britain 1830-1910*, Oxford, 1999.

Yelton, Michael, *Anglican Papalism: A History 1900-1960*, Canterbury, 2005.